MW00635748

ACCLAIM FOR
IF NOT YOU, THEN WHO?

"Jesse Harless has written a true master guide to recovery. His personal story is raw and deeply revealing. He could have easily justified a lifetime of self-destruction, wallowing in the pain of an unfair childhood. Instead, he took that pain and transformed himself into a true sober warrior, using his unique abilities to help others. There are many paths to recovery from addiction, but they all start with a true acknowledgment of pain. Jesse could have stopped there, and this book would still have great value. But he has created a true roadmap to healthy sobriety by taking certain actions, digging deeply into the source of pain, giving the reader real growth exercises, and showing them how to be accountable for the results. This book should be on every shelf, whether you are a recovery professional or someone seeking to build a better life."

Charlie Engle, ultra marathon runner,
author of *Running Man*

"Jesse uses his inspiring personal story to provide a method of transformational change that will be of benefit to anyone, at any point, on a journey of recovery. The FEARS recovery toolkit and the inclusion of specific action steps make this a book that individuals, clinicians, and others on the support teams of individuals can all benefit from. All clinicians working with those in recovery should be familiar with the FEARS recovery toolkit and recommend this book and its action steps to those they support."

Dr. Cynthia Whitaker, President & CEO,
Greater Nashua Mental Health

"*If Not You, Then Who?* is a remarkable story of Jesse Harless's battle with addiction and his formula for finding success in recovery. He's living proof of what's possible for someone in recovery who follows their heart. This book is a new paradigm of what's possible for all of us."

Hal Elrod, international best-selling author,
The Miracle Morning

"Jesse Harless's powerful story of addiction and recovery would be enough to inspire and motivate others dealing with similar struggles. But he also brings to this book a practical step-by-step recovery plan to put that inspiration and motivation into action."

Lisa Smith, best-selling author,
Girl Walks Out of a Bar

"Jesse Harless is a gifted storyteller able to share his own 'gritty' recovery journey and his intuitive life lessons in a way that invites us all to suit up and show up once more in the exciting game of life!"

Jean LaCour, PhD, founder of ICARE
(International Center of Addiction and Recovery Education)

"If Not You, Then Who? is an absolute must-read for anyone who has struggled with any kind of addiction, be it to a substance, to self-doubt, to a toxic behavior or to living in fear. Jesse Harless shares powerfully and beautifully how he transmuted his own past trauma and has elevated his recovery from drugs and alcohol to living a transformed life of service and connection to his highest calling. He teaches you how to do the same! This book is a recovery bible for anyone looking to change their life and work through your FEARS in a whole new capacity that will give rise to your flourishing. If you are ready to reimagine and rewrite the next chapter of your life, you must read and implement If Not You, Then Who?"

Julie Reisler, Master Transformational Coach, Author,
Speaker, Georgetown University Faculty

www.WorkOnYourFears.com

Copyright © 2021 by Jesse Harless

All rights reserved. No part of this publication may be reproduced, distributed, or transmitted in any form or by any means, including photocopying, recording, or other electronic or mechanical methods, without the prior written permission of the publisher, except in the case of brief quotations embodied in reviews and certain other noncommercial uses permitted by copyright law.

Published by Entrepreneurs in Recovery, www.jesseharless.com

Front-cover design: Diane McIntosh

Photo of Jesse Harless: April Piotrowski

Interior design: Dino Marino, www.dinomarino.com

HeartMath is a registered trademark of Quantum Intech, Inc. For all HeartMath trademarks go to www. heartmath.com/trademarks

ISBN: 978-1-7335316-1-0

IF NOT YOU, THEN WHO?

HARNESS YOUR STRENGTHS TO SHIFT
FROM ADDICTION TO ABUNDANCE

JESSE HARLESS

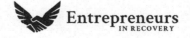

DISCLAIMER

This book is meant to provide helpful information about the subject addressed and should not be used as a diagnosis, prognosis, or treatment recommendation. Please consult your health-care provider or medical practitioner before starting any new health program or treatment. The author is not liable for any action taken by a reader based upon this information.

ACKNOWLEDGMENTS

My thanks go to my mother, Deborah Harless, who has always supported, guided, and cheered me on. I would not be the man I am today without your love and encouragement.

Thank you to my brother Justin. You were my first mentor and helped me through many difficult periods. You are an angel.

Thank you to my brother Derek who has found his way to recovery and is now giving back in a major way. I appreciate all your encouragement and support.

My deepest appreciation goes out to all of my friends, mentors, and people in recovery who have helped me more than they will ever know.

A special thank you to Amanda Rooker for your endless dedication and support throughout the entire writing of this book.

If Not You, Then Who? is for all those continuing the path of becoming the best version of themselves.

CONTENTS

INTRODUCTION

On the morning of December 22, 2005, I was four days sober and scared shitless. I had slept over at my brother Justin's house the night before, and that morning he held back tears as he helped with my tie. I was to appear that day before a federal judge in a U.S. district court for using the mail to obtain pharmaceutical drugs. Justin drove my mother, his wife Julie, and me to the post office in Manchester, New Hampshire, where I was arranged to be detained.

As I made my way inside, I was met by the federal agent who'd arrested me nine months prior. He handcuffed me and took me through a side exit where his cruiser awaited to drive me to the federal courthouse in Concord. I was brought to a cell where I had plenty of time to think about where my addiction had taken me. I couldn't help but think about how this whole mess could have been avoided. Now my family was at the front and center of it. Despite my belief that my choices were only affecting me, the reality was my addiction was affecting everyone around me, most of all the ones I loved.

That day was fifteen years ago, but it feels like yesterday. Although I didn't know it at the time, it was the beginning of a journey of recovery that would transform my adversities into a message of hope for those facing similar circumstances.

One thing I've learned about true recovery is that it transforms your whole life. Choosing recovery gives us the opportunity to co-create a life of health, wellness, purpose, and fulfillment.

Many of us live by the scripts of old stories and past traumas that keep us trapped in our own minds. When we're in active addiction, we are in survival mode. We spend every day looking to get our next fix, whether that's food, technology, people-pleasing, drugs, alcohol, sex, fear, power, gambling, or any other method of escaping our lives. Addiction becomes the perpetual loop that ultimately leads to an unfulfilled life and an early death.

On our journey of recovery, the first thing we must achieve is freedom from the bondage of our addiction, otherwise known as sobriety. This freedom is foundational. I will share more about the ways people achieve this freedom later on.

But for true recovery, sobriety is not enough. The second freedom essential to recovery is the freedom to co-create a life of meaning and purpose. Living a life of meaning and purpose can feel like it's reserved for a select few. I attempted to find this freedom throughout my life, but trauma, low self-worth, anxiety, and addiction continued to reverse my efforts. I consumed, drank, smoked, sniffed, swallowed, and injected substances to drown my fear, insecurity, and pain. I moved from one addiction to the next, hoping to find relief. When I did make some progress, it was quickly canceled out by negative thoughts, shame, anxiety, depression, and a feeling that I didn't belong.

These experiences didn't go away just because I found freedom from my addictions. I had to continue to be willing and open to learn and implement new tools for healing in order to feel comfortable in my own skin. While sobriety is about surviving, recovery is about thriving.

What you'll find in this book is my own personal story followed by my recovery toolkit that you can apply to your own life, starting today. This toolkit is based on fifteen years of personal experience in addiction recovery and what I've witnessed working with thousands of people also in recovery.

I've learned that recovery is holistic because we all have a physical, emotional, mental, and spiritual body. Because we are multidimensional beings, there are multiple pathways to recovery. The beauty of recovery is in the diversity of its solutions. For example, my friend George found long-term recovery using the 12 Steps, combined with a daily yoga and meditation practice. I know others who choose fitness, art, music therapy, somatic experiencing, holistic health practices, recovery coaching, ecotherapy, faith, service work, and various other practices to create their pathway to recovery.[1]

If you're currently struggling with addiction, you have probably already discovered that addiction can be a very difficult and confusing topic for those who haven't experienced it. We all tend to judge a person by their current actions and behaviors. This is understandable, but in doing so we fail to see the layers of trauma and challenging life experiences that shaped this person's world. If you experienced what that person experienced, who's to say you wouldn't behave the same way?

Don't ask a person, "What's wrong with you?"
Ask, "What happened to you?"

Gabor Mate, MD

Oftentimes the greatest stigma exists inside of the recovery community. People who are recovering often judge another's individual path to recovery. How does a person who has been through the messiness of addiction judge another's path to recovery? This often happens because of their own fear or perception.

HONORING EVERY PATH TO RECOVERY ELIMINATES THIS STIGMA.

The stigma and negative attitudes surrounding addiction and mental health are killing thousands of people. That's why we need to hear from the millions of people living a life of recovery. My hope is many will read this book and say to themselves, "How can I share my recovery story?" It's time for us to stop hiding.

As someone who has struggled with addiction and mental health conditions for most of my life, this book was written for me as much as it was for you. I know I'm not alone when I say finding recovery was a matter of life and death. There's no going back to the way things used to be. I was broken, bruised, and near death at the end of my run with my addictions. The circumstances of my life made me willing to change.

In part one, I share my story from the beginning. You will learn how addiction played a role in my family, my choices, and my life circumstances. You will learn how I found recovery and how I trusted my intuition to guide me through the unknown.

You may or may not relate with certain parts of my story or identify with some of the feelings I describe. Maybe this book was given to you as a gift or it randomly appeared during a search. Perhaps you found this book lying around your sober living residence or at your treatment center.

You might even know someone else who would benefit from reading my story, since we are all affected by the damage addiction causes.

Regardless of your situation, I've learned that sharing my story with others causes a ripple effect of healing. The same can be true for you: When you share your story of adversity, resilience, and recovery, you give people permission to share their own story. When you help one person, you are helping the collective human family.

In part two, you'll discover the recovery toolkit I used to work through fear, adversity, shame, and self-doubt to help me co-create a life I'm passionate about living. Recovery is a lifelong journey. It requires consistent action. But which behaviors support long-term success? As I experienced new addictions and poor habits along my recovery journey, I researched new ways to evolve and learn from teachers. I experimented with tools, techniques, and habits to piece together a recovery toolkit. The recovery toolkit I developed is called FEARS:

- **F**ocus
- **E**levate
- **A**ppreciate
- **R**esilience
- **S**elf-Care

I chose to use the acronym FEARS despite some misgivings about the word *fear*. Fear is not always a bad thing. Fear can actually guide us in achieving our full potential in life because on the other side of fear lies what we truly desire.

With FEARS, we can overcome our fear.

Some of these methods are unconventional and even a little weird. But in order to grow, we must be willing to try new things. Pain makes us willing to grow. At the same time, it's perfectly okay to be exactly where you are at this very moment. My recommendation is to take what you need from this book and leave the rest. I often read an entire book and only remember one key idea or concept, but that one key concept helps me take inspired action to change my life.

Our deepest fear is not that we are inadequate.
Our deepest fear is that we are powerful beyond measure.
It is our light, not our darkness, that most frightens us.

Marianne Williamson

Addiction awakened me to a need for serious healing and unlearning. Recovery is not always about learning something new, but unlearning old ideas, beliefs, and stories that no longer serve you. I had to let go of people's opinions about what's best for my life and rise above the stigma of being labeled an "addict" or a felon.

Today I choose not to be silent. I've lost too many friends and family members to mental health conditions and addiction.

A wise mentor once told me that not sharing my story with the world is causing more suffering in the world. So now I share my story with you with the hope that together we will inspire millions of others to find recovery.

PART ONE:

MY STORY

CHAPTER 1

MY FIRST DRUG WAS FANTASY

The first few months of my life started in Lawrence, Massachusetts. Addiction was common in my family. It's not something to be proud of. It just is what it is. Times were different during my parents' generation. My mother smoked Marlboro cigarettes, drank brandy, and sipped wine during her pregnancy with me. My father smoked pot, drank alcohol, and did the "occasional" line of cocaine. His addiction to harder drugs began when he was in the army. When my father was discharged, he turned to cocaine, marijuana, and alcohol. His heroin usage overseas did not come without consequences, as he had acquired Hepatitis C. When my father met my mother, he promised her that he would no longer use hard drugs. His addiction didn't become a problem until we moved to a beautiful home in New Hampshire.

The year 1986 was a tough one for my mother. Her father had a heart attack, her mother had to be placed in a nursing home, and my father was sent to a veterans' hospital to detox from drugs and alcohol. On top of all this, at age three, I was rushed to the hospital for a double hernia that required surgery. The stress and tension in my environment developed into *dis-ease* in my little body. After hitting another hard "bottom," my father entered detox again.

Then my father seemed to bounce back. He took my family and me to Cape Cod on vacation. My father joined Alcoholics Anonymous and had a sponsor named Charlie. All was well for a time until my father relapsed with cocaine and alcohol, which caused him to lose his job at the post office. With money being the number one stressor, my mother made the decision to leave my father. She was now a young single mother with three young boys to raise. My father moved into a trailer park with his brother, who was also an alcoholic.

The last family gathering I can remember was for my fourth birthday party at Chuck E. Cheese. I still remember running through the mouse holes and jumping into four feet of plastic balls. Soon after my birthday, my father was gone for good.

My father leaving was my first memory of abandonment. My behavior changed dramatically after he left. I would stab couches with knives and light objects on fire inside our home. It took several decades of poor decisions for me to recognize the profound impact losing a parent has on a child. Painful experiences early on in life often go unrecognized, but we will have to address these issues during our recovery process. Today we know that trauma in early childhood can lead to addiction in young adulthood.[2]

My father left at the most impressionable time of childhood. What developed in me was an unconscious belief that I was unlovable and that it was not okay to be myself: There must be something wrong with me if my dad left and never came back. Today I know that addiction took my dad from me. I've spoken with many people who have gone through traumatic life experiences who have not yet realized that trauma doesn't always go away on its own. Trauma can become stuck or immobilized when we don't deal with it.[3] If left unresolved, a person may develop addictive tendencies with food, relationships, drugs, alcohol, and more. Adverse childhood experiences, such as a father or mother leaving at a young age, can even impact the nervous system.[4]

It's easy for us to disregard trauma and the impact it has on our life. You might have heard a loved one say, "You need to toughen up," "You're too sensitive," or "Life's hard; get used to it." We are often programmed by our school system and authority figures to believe life is about competition and survival of the fittest. The truth is that unless we have dealt with them, old traumas are still playing out in our adult lives in subtle ways, such as overeating, overspending, or watching hours of television to tune out. These experiences are keeping us from reaching our highest potential.

After my father left, the world seemed to come crashing down on my family. My mother put the house up for sale since there was little money coming in. She sold her new car to keep up with the bills. My father found a new job but was fired from it. If that wasn't enough, my mother went to the doctor for pain she was experiencing and was told she had a large tumor in her pelvic area. The doctors told her to prepare for the worst.

She had tremendous stress and anxiety during the five weeks before her surgery. She was faced with thoughts of dying from cancer and leaving three boys with no father and no mother. My mom was so panicked she would keep her lights on when she went to bed at night. Between the stress of selling a home, looking for a new place to live, and the possibility of cancer, my mom had to get rid of my dog. First, it was my dad, now my dog. I was sent to live with my uncle, and my brothers were sent to live with my grandparents.

On September 16, 1987, my mom went in for surgery to remove the tumor. The surgery ended up being a success. Her left ovary was removed, and the tumor never returned.

A few weeks after the surgery, my mother got news that my father was in a horrific car accident in West Virginia. During a night of drinking and partying, he crashed his car into the side of a mountain. He was in a coma for twenty-two days and suffered severe brain damage. At one point, there was even a question of whether to keep him on life support. I was too young at the time for my mom to tell me what had happened, but my heart could sense something was wrong.

Throughout these early experiences, I relied heavily on my very first addiction: thumb-sucking. Thumb-sucking brought me ease and comfort even inside my mother's womb. Thumb-sucking was a coping mechanism for the stress and pain I felt about my father leaving. It provided relief when I felt scared, such as the time our apartment was broken into, and our VCR was stolen.

My attempts to hide thumb-sucking from people weren't working. My kindergarten teacher, Mr. Hardgraves, insisted on holding me back from the first grade because of my obsessive thumb-sucking. Thumb-sucking is not a problem for a one-year-old, but I was now six. I became a functioning thumb-sucker. The embarrassment of family and friends helped me quit thumb-sucking by the age of ten, but I soon found another coping mechanism for fear and anxiety.

Sugar, fast food, and sodas. During my preteen years, you could find me at the convenience store daily purchasing Laffy Taffy, Nerds, Now and Later, and Coca-Cola. Because I was a picky eater and a pain in the ass to my single mother, she gave me money for fast food. I would eat small extra-cheese pizzas multiple times a week. I loved coffee frappes and made them as often as possible. My brother worked at Little Caesars, so I had cheesy breadsticks with the dipping sauce anytime I wanted. Eating this way led to chronic issues with asthma, sinus infections, allergies, and colds. My mother was not aware of the effects foods like dairy and white sugar can have on a child's immune system.

I visited the hospital many times as a child. At age ten, I had a sort of heart attack during class and was brought to Boston Children's Hospital. I was required to wear a heart monitor the entire summer. Wearing a heart monitor meant I had to miss being selected for the ten-year-old's all-star team for baseball, trips to Canobie Lake with friends, and anything that would cause my heart to become too excited. For the first time in my life, I had a fear of dying.

This all changed when my new friend Matt moved into my apartment complex. Matt and I were inseparable. We went to the same school, listened to the same music, and played sports and video games daily. I even dated his sister at one point. Matt and I would go on fishing escapades often. One time, we decided to fish for salmon by a large dam on the Merrimack River. An alarm sounded, which meant the dam was opening, and thousands of gallons of water would soon cover the rocks we were currently standing on. We didn't pay attention, though; we were determined to catch fish. In no time at all, we found ourselves unable to escape the rising water as we were pulled down the raging river, fishing poles and all. Adventures like this were common.

One day, Matt told me he was moving. Now another person I cared about was leaving. Even though he only moved to a different part of the city, he might as well have moved to a different country. After that, I started to spend all of my time after school and on the weekends glued to a computer screen. When my mother started her second job at a cable company, my whole world seemed to change overnight. High-speed internet would launch me into a new world of addiction.

It is often said that people with addiction lead a double life. My double life started at age twelve when we upgraded to high-speed internet. This new world allowed me hours upon hours of internet games and porn uninterrupted. No one knew I was watching internet porn on a regular basis because I kept it hidden. This is not uncommon. Gary Wilson, author of the book *Your Brain on Porn*, states, "Most users start watching porn by puberty, when their brains are at their peak of plasticity and most vulnerable to addiction and rewiring."[5] I was hooked on internet porn. Research has shown internet porn can cause trauma in young boys. Exposure to internet pornography at a young age can be traumatic because we are experiencing sexually explicit scenes before we are old enough to experience sex ourselves.[6]

Living in a fantasy world was great until it was time for responsibilities, relationships, and school. Being in my bedroom for six to eight hours at a time caused me to miss many social activities during high school. Isolation became a close friend of mine. I stopped seeking relationships outside of my online world. Why would I need to connect with others when I could get super-large hits of dopamine watching pornography and playing games? What started out as pleasurable experiences soon turned into feelings of guilt, shame, and remorse. Whenever I experienced a painful event, I would turn to internet pornography. Over time, I would watch more illicit content to get the same effect as before. Something similar happens with drug addiction. In the beginning, the first dose is adequate, but then as a person's tolerance increases, one dose turns into three, six, or nine doses just to feel normal again. Internet pornography affects the same parts of the brain as cocaine, which eventually became my drug of choice in my early twenties.[7] But for the time being, self-medicating my feelings with fantasy was working just fine.

FANTASY BECAME MY DRUG OF CHOICE.

Four years after my father left, my mother dated a man I looked up to and admired. He was tall and confident, and he drove a white Cadillac with a cell phone inside it. Ironically, he frequented the same bar my father once drank in called the Club. One morning I walked into his bedroom and saw my mother on the bed with sunglasses on. I knew something was wrong. I asked her to remove her sunglasses, which revealed her huge black eye. My first thought was to hurt this man. I knew where he kept his guns, and it was all I could do not to grab one. My mom explained how she was struck in the eye during a bar fight at the Club. Not long after this incident, my mom left him. He did not keep in touch, which I think is normal. He was the closest thing I had to a real father growing up.

I want to take a moment to share that I did have many unforgettable memories during childhood. There were wonderful birthdays and Christmases, thanks to my mom's tireless dedication to her three sons. Being the youngest meant I always got amazing presents. My brothers would do anything for me, especially Justin. Justin supported me through youth sports and life experiences. He became a father figure to me even though he was only eight years older than me. I was blessed to have him as a male role model. Because my mother worked full time, I had freedom kids today can only dream about. I would spend hours in the woods looking for treasure since we lived next to a state forest. Nature became a place of wonder, healing, and excitement. There was so much to explore and so little time. My addiction to a computer screen would soon replace this habit I so enjoyed.

Ironically, I was a late bloomer. While my friends started hitting puberty around thirteen, I started the process at seventeen. This only made matters worse. I often felt feelings of loneliness and awkwardness as a teenager. I made attempts to adapt to the high school environment by playing sports during my freshman and sophomore years. Sophomore year I decided to play lacrosse. During practice, which was a mix of varsity and junior varsity players, a senior player decided to run at me when I had my head down attempting to scoop up a lacrosse ball. He laid a nasty hit that put me on my back with snot bubbles. I got up, sore and embarrassed. No one was there to comfort me or comment on what had happened. I was completely devastated, but I tried not to show it. My teammates no longer respected me. I felt they had abandoned me on the field that day. The next year I quit all sports.

Despite what was happening in my world, my grandfather was there to make me laugh and take life less seriously. He always had a sunny disposition and was good for a joke at any moment. Henry Ruiter— or Grampy, as we called him—was one of the greatest men I have ever known. Grampy fought in World War II for the U.S. Navy on the USS Cronin; he was also a Golden Gloves boxer in Lowell, Massachusetts. Grampy lived next to my high school, so every day I would walk over to his apartment so he could drive me around to deliver newspapers after school. This gave him an opportunity to smoke cigarettes and hide them from his wife.

He shared just one story with me about World War II during our drives together, and that was for a paper I wrote for school. I realized Grampy had done things to survive in the war that he'd rather not talk about. When I was sixteen years old, Grampy gave me his car after he was diagnosed with terminal lung cancer. My brother Justin and I got to visit him the night he died in his apartment. Justin and I had a moment together to laugh and cry as we arrived on the 4th floor of Grampy's apartment. Grampy would have wanted us to laugh even at his funeral. The world lost a great man that night.

After Grampy's death, my social anxiety and depression increased. I did not attend my prom and ate alone outside of the cafeteria my entire senior year because of my fear, anxiety, and depression. During senior year, I was late so many times my high school set up an intervention. When seniors got the last week of school off, I showed up to every class to make sure I got my diploma. When it came time for college, my mother was a major influence because I would be a first-generation college student in our family. My mother sacrificed everything for her three children. She instilled Christian values in me at a young age, which laid the foundation for my own spirituality as an adult. If it were up to me, I would have opted out of college and isolated myself playing online games and living in my safe, comfortable fantasy world.

I chose to attend a small school that was not too far from home. Plymouth State University had around four to five thousand students. Naturally, I enrolled in the computer science program since I loved spending all my time on the computer. A few weeks into the semester, the 9/11 attacks happened in the U.S. I was eating breakfast when I saw the video of the planes hitting the Twin Towers. I remember the college campus having an eerie quietness to it as, one by one, classes were canceled. A few of my classmates lost loved ones during 9/11. It was a tragic day for America.

My intention was to make college work, but it didn't take long to discover that college life offered more than just academics. Smoking weed and drinking alcohol on the weekends became a common occurrence. Weekends started on Thursdays in college, but for me they moved to Wednesdays. There was no shortage of partying my first semester.

One night, I decided to walk the streets with a cup in my hand and a bottle of rum mixed with orange soda in my backpack. I asked my roommate to join me. A few streets later, I spotted a state trooper driving up the road and told my roommate I was going to run for it. My roommate decided not to run, so I decided to stay put and play it cool. After passing us, the trooper quickly U-turned and got out of her vehicle. She asked what was in my cup, and I told the truth. I suddenly realized I had a bag of weed in my pocket. To my surprise, she did not find the weed during her search since I had it in the front pocket of my shorts. We were arrested and placed in her car. I was charged for an open container in public and fined $500. I knew the situation could have been much worse. It was the first in a series of signposts that drugs, alcohol, and managing my own life were going to be issues for me.

I stopped attending my morning classes because I was too hungover. I sold my textbooks for weed and pizza. While other students seemed to "manage" their drug and alcohol use, I was failing. I failed all of my classes first semester, including a one-credit class called Introduction to College. I'm pretty sure you pass this class by listening to a person talk about college. Nonetheless, I failed it. To make matters worse, I was caught for plagiarism in my Introduction to Literature class. I copied and pasted a paragraph from the internet and used it in one of my papers. This landed me in front of a review board to decide the penalty. The board's decision was to give me a failing grade for the class.

Despite my 0.6 GPA and failing all of my classes, the school let me back for a second semester. Once again, I had every intention of turning things around. I lived next to the school's beautiful library and told myself I would visit there every week. I needed A's and B's to get my GPA high enough to stay in school. I ended up getting a B in two classes, but it was not enough to get me off probation.

I came home to live with my mother. I felt ashamed of the $19,000 student loan debt and for flunking out. I found a job at Staples and began making plans to get my life in order. I quickly became friends with coworkers and people who smoked weed and drank. When I wasn't partying, I was on the computer.

On August 27, 2003, I came home from work to find my mom panic-stricken. She told me my father had passed away earlier in the day. This was a man I had spoken to on the phone only a few times since he left when I was four, and I hadn't seen him for sixteen years. I felt resentful, frustrated, and angry. I had so many unexpressed feelings. Why did life have to be so painful? I stormed out of the house and phoned one of my new friends.

Later that night, I was at a small gathering where cocaine was being passed around. I had never tried cocaine before, but I knew it was my father's drug of choice. When the cocaine got to me, I didn't hesitate. I would chase the feelings I got from those first few lines for the next three years of my life. Despite the fact that my father just died, I had never felt this good. For the first time in my young adult life, I felt a deep connection with the people around me. I felt powerful. I felt free. I felt love. Once the drug wore off, I had to find a way to feel this good again.

My mom received a large sum of money from my father's passing and purchased a trailer home. It was nice to have a safe place to rest my head after my trips to Lowell, Massachusetts, to score drugs with a friend. I began to pawn my belongings to have money for gas and drugs. I once pawned a bird cage for a measly ten dollars that was so big I could fit myself into it.

What I didn't know about my friend is that he had an addiction to heroin. As my money grew shorter, I had trouble purchasing cocaine. He suggested for a fraction of the cost, we could purchase a bundle of heroin. I told him I would snort it but never, I mean never, shoot it!

After a few weeks of snorting heroin, I showed up at his home and saw a rubber band, a needle, and bags of heroin. Despite my initial protestations, a few minutes later I had strapped up the rubber band and let him shoot heroin into my arm. Within seconds I felt a warm feeling running throughout my entire body. My eyelids felt heavy, and there was a sudden rush of euphoria. Within another few minutes, I was nauseous and ran to the bathroom.

I promised myself I would only shoot up occasionally. As things grew worse, I saw my friend withering away from his daily heroin use. He eventually got arrested. My friend had been the only person I felt safe to use drugs with. What the hell was I going to do now?

I quit heroin and cocaine cold turkey and replaced them with alcohol. Drinking alcohol every night and isolating myself on the computer became my new routine. No one knew the last nine months had been filled with cocaine and heroin use. I went out looking for a job since I hadn't been working the entire time. During my first job search, I stopped for gas. I decided to open my trunk and found a needle inside. I immediately felt sick to my stomach and discarded it.

A few streets away from the station was a shopping plaza. I made my way into a wireless phone store to ask if they were hiring. A few weeks later I returned and got the job. Despite using heroin and cocaine only a few weeks before, I now found myself selling cell phones. I enjoyed the thrill of selling to customers and quickly became a top salesperson.

As time passed, I became close friends with my coworker Mike. Mike was the most laid-back person I'd ever met. He was smart, funny, and artistic. I felt comfortable enough to share with him my recent struggles with heroin and cocaine use. He listened to me with compassion and without judgment. By this point, I was only drinking and smoking weed once in a while. Then one day I was offered Vicodin. I justified that pain killers were much safer than heroin. I began researching on the internet how I could order Vicodin myself. This decision would change my life forever.

CHAPTER 2

CHAPTER 2

I NEVER MADE IT TO DISNEY WORLD

Taking Vicodin was much safer than driving to Lowell for shady street deals. Plus, pills never got in the way of my daily life. I continued to excel at work, which kept my mind busy and prevented me from obsessing about the pills. Only when I left work did I need to fix my discomfort and self-medicate. My feelings of anxiety or depression were quickly erased with alcohol and pills, but before long, I needed more.

ADDICTION IS ALL ABOUT MORE.

In my search to ease the pain, I found an online source that would ship prescription pain medication if I sent them a money order. I was desperate and willing to give it a try. I didn't want any packages being delivered to my mother's trailer, so I had them sent to a local UPS Store.

My first trip to send a money order was nerve-wracking. I intuitively knew this was a bad idea, but I still sent the money. After a few weeks of no response, I began to think I had been ripped off. Then one day my phone rang. It was the UPS Store telling me they received a package. Was this really happening? I picked up the package and drove away with anticipation. When I opened the package, I found a sealed bottle, and inside were dozens of Vicodin. I was blown away.

I eagerly waited for my workday to end so I could consume these little blue pills with a few beers while getting lost in online games. Once the pills were gone, I sent money again. This cycle went on for many months. Most of my paycheck was now being spent on pills. I decided to investigate if Oxycontin was an option to order. I knew Oxys were more similar to heroin. Yes, Oxys were also available. When the first package arrived, there was just a magazine inside. When I flipped through it, I found a cutout with a bag of 20 small pills in it. Things were about to change.

The packages were almost always different. The pills might be in a magazine, a sealed bottle, or even hidden inside a VHS tape. At this point I was drinking and consuming dozens of pills on a weekly basis. As my tolerance grew, I continued to push the limits. One day, I decided to swallow and snort several Oxys mixed with alcohol. The next morning was unbearable. The pain in my head was worse than anything I'd experienced in my life. I didn't move out of my bed for fifteen hours. My mother would be home soon, and I wasn't going to let her see me like this.

Despite my nauseousness and excruciating headache, I left the trailer. I drove around my town for hours hoping to feel "normal" again. It was so dark that night. A sense of deep loneliness and despair came over me. Music only made things worse. I drove in silence. I had a strong realization I was going to die if I kept this up.

By the next morning, I was off to work and feeling better. Remorse, depression, and pain are short-lived when you're in active addiction. I was now surrounded by customers complaining about their broken car chargers, shitty battery life, or dropped calls, which allowed me to get outside of my head. Despite my daily drug habit, I never missed a day of work. I was a "functioning" addict.

As my addiction progressed, Mike offered me a chance to move to Florida. In my mind, if I could escape New Hampshire, I could quit my addiction to pills and start over. I told him I was in. Things were looking up. A few weeks before I was scheduled to move, I decided to go to Walmart to pick up some supplies. As I walked around the store, my phone rang. It was the call I was longing for: the UPS Store telling me my package was in! A package to make me feel normal again. Nothing made me happier. I often experienced a high just before picking up my package, a feeling only surpassed by the high itself.

I answered my phone, "Hello."

"Is this Jesse Harless?"

"Speaking."

"Yes, Jesse, this is the UPS Store. I want to let you know that your package was not delivered here. It was sent to the post office."

I immediately knew something was terribly wrong.

"The post office?" I said with dismay.

"Yeah, the Plaistow post office has your package."

"Okay, thank you."

I should have trusted my intuition. I should have just gone home and forgotten all about it. But I needed those pills. It was a nonnegotiable. My craving felt like it was beyond this world. I spent the next twenty-five minutes driving in silence.

When I arrived at the post office, it happened to be empty of customers. I walked up to the counter and signed for my package. I walked out the two sets of doors and was making my way to the car when I was suddenly swarmed by police officers. I was handcuffed and brought back inside the post office. I happened to have $800 on me I'd won at the Mohegan Sun Casino for my twenty-first birthday a few nights before, which didn't help my situation. The agent asked questions to figure out who I was, who I was dealing to, and who else was involved. They had a hard time believing me because I lied and told them the pills were for my ADHD and back soreness. They weren't buying any of it. The truth was I really did consume all of the pills. I was handed a warrant to search my home. The problem was that it wasn't my home. What would I tell my mother? I told them I lived with a single mom who experienced a difficult life living with alcoholics and drug addicts. I didn't want to make her life any harder than it had been.

An agent drove me in my car, and a black SUV followed behind, as we headed to the trailer. When we walked inside, I told my mom the gentlemen were here to purchase my snowboard. She bought the lie. The officers seized my computer and several receipts from my room. It didn't take long. Expecting to be taken off to jail, I was shocked when the agents started heading back to their vehicle. I asked, "What's going to happen now?" A federal agent handed me a card and told me to keep in touch. They were letting me go. I told them I was moving to Florida in two weeks, and they simply said to call them when I got down there. What the hell was going on?

A person in active addiction will do anything to protect their problem from being discovered. I held off a few days, but I finally told Mike what had happened. I convinced him I was going to be okay. I failed to mention the next package that was due to arrive at the UPS Store. But who cared? We would be in Florida soon enough.

We finally made our long drive down to Florida. It was 2005, a few months before Hurricane Katrina. I was ready to turn my life around. The last three years with drugs and alcohol were a messy blur. Now I had a fresh start. The ad on the internet made our new place in Orlando look like a paradise. I made a call to the federal agent to check in. It would be the last time I would speak to him for eight months.

By the time we made it to St. Augustine, I was already getting high again. It was a sign of things to come. We were ready to start work as soon as we arrived, but our new boss, Mark, told us the store was still being completed. Mike and I got paid for a short period of time to do nothing. We visited the beaches and enjoyed the hot spring days. I purchased a plant and a turtle despite not being able to take care of myself. I was drinking, smoking weed, and using pain pills on a regular basis, but I seemed to be managing. I told myself that I was fine as long as I stayed away from cocaine and heroin. This lasted for about four months.

One night, smoking a cigarette outside my local bar, a woman asked if I did cocaine. I knew cocaine was off limits because with it, all of my previous experiences had gone to shit. I would end up pawning all of my stuff to chase this high. I told her no, which brought some momentary pride. About two shots later, we spoke during our next cigarette break. I asked her why she asked me that question. Next thing I knew I was on my way to purchase the cocaine. When it arrived, I offered to share, but she refused. Great, I thought, more for me! I could do some now and save the rest for tomorrow. Within an hour I had finished the bag, despite having to work the next day. I went to bed and rolled up in a fetal position with a pillow over my head. There was no sleep that night.

I was off and running again. For some odd reason, our apartment bathroom had two large mirrors in it. Every morning, I managed to avoid looking at my reflection. When I did catch a glimpse of myself, I was disgusted. I was strung out, malnourished, and sleep deprived. When I took a shower, the water felt like nails on my skin. My diet consisted mainly of ramen noodles or nachos at the bar.

As my addiction spiraled out of control, I would arrive at the ale house earlier and earlier to get a drink. My "friends" who were drinking and doing cocaine seemed to manage okay. Why couldn't I?

One night, a gentleman sat next to me at the bar. He grabbed a napkin and began writing. He slid the napkin over, which said, "Read this book," and left the bar before I could say anything. I lost the napkin that night, but I remembered what it said: *The Power of Positive Thinking* by Norman Vincent Peale.

A few days later, while I was walking through a flea market, I saw a red book. The author was Norman Vincent Peale. The book was called The *True Joy of Positive Living*. I began reading it, and I was moved by the author's life story and uplifting message. I felt a small glimmer of hope inside, something I hadn't felt since arriving in Florida. I wondered if there was more to life than what I was living. Despite my new revelations, this new book quickly became a place to snort cocaine from.

I always found a way to keep my drug habit alive, even as money grew short. Working two jobs to support my habit was not enough. After a long night of partying at my dealer's home, I had not slept and was wide awake at 8:00 a.m. All of a sudden there was a knock at the door. All around me were paraphernalia and empty bags. I was freaking out. I hid every piece of evidence I could find, stuffing things between the couch cushions. There was a second knock at the door. I snuck a peek out the window, only to see a cable guy waiting to talk to someone. Thank God! When the cable guy left, I began the drive back to my place. I was extremely paranoid and depressed as I approached the toll booth. I can only imagine what the woman at the booth must have thought of my appearance. As I entered our apartment, a look of utter disgust and disappointment was on my roommate's face. No words were exchanged.

Hurricane Katrina was all over the news by this time. I would drink at the bar and watch as the storm grew closer. The day after Katrina hit, our street was flooded. Because I had to get to work to support my drug habit, I was determined to drive through it. Apparently, my blue Daewoo is not a jet ski. Halfway through the flood water, my engine seized. Luckily my neighbors helped push my car out of the flooded street. The Daewoo was dead.

I was scheduled to return to New Hampshire in September to celebrate my brother Justin's wedding. He asked me to be his best man. I had waited my whole life for this moment. This was the man who came to my baseball and football games as a kid and supported me throughout my life. But Justin did not know the extent of my addiction, and I wasn't sure how I was going to cope without using back home.

Justin had arranged for my brother Derek to stay in the same hotel room with me the night before his wedding. Derek was someone I had used drugs with in the past. Our night started out with a few beers out on the patio. Before I knew it, an eight ball of cocaine was brought out. Here I was, on the night before the most important day of Justin's life, and I'm about to get high on cocaine. It wasn't long before the bag was finished.

There were at least two hundred people in attendance the next day. I don't think I slept an hour. As we made our way to the procession, a waiter was serving Jack Daniels and Coke. I drank one, and then another. I must have had at least three drinks, but I was far from drunk. It was just enough to make me feel something. When the time came to present my speech, I still had the capacity to find love for a man who had always been there for me. My speech brought Justin to tears. We embraced each other and had a good cry. I felt safe in that moment. Little did he know the hell I was living on the inside. A day or so later, I flew back to Orlando.

It was now time to get help. I made an appointment at the Florida Hospital Orlando with an intention to tell the doctor I had a serious drug problem. As I sat in the parking lot the day of my appointment, I thought about driving away. Then a thought came, What if I could get medication to make me feel better? Yeah, that's it. I will get some Adderall.

I sat down in Dr. Le's office. When he began to check vital signs and stick the scope up my nose, I waited for him to see holes in my nose or something that would indicate I had a problem. "Please tell me I have a problem, Dr. Le!" I thought desperately. Instead, he asked why I came to see him. I said I was having a hard time focusing, and I felt depressed. I told him ADHD medication would help. When he started to explain the lengthy process and tests involved to get medication, I knew I was screwed. I needed something right now.

He then asked me a question that baffled me. He said, "Can I pray for you?" I couldn't believe it. Here was a doctor of medicine asking to pray for me. There's no way this was standard protocol, but I was desperate, so I said yes. He said a short prayer and then proceeded to look up something on his computer. He found a meeting at a church not far from Orlando. He wrote down the address on the back of his card and handed it to me.

Although I walked out of the hospital empty-handed, I had a good feeling about the meeting. I made it through the rest of the day sober. The meeting at the church was a gathering for young people looking to make new connections. It wasn't what I was expecting, but I made a connection with a woman who told me to come back to an event led by a pastor named Joel C. Hunter. A few days later, I drove back to the church to hear his talk. The pastor described a moment at his mother's funeral after everyone had gone home. While standing by her casket, he began to weep uncontrollably and started to fall backwards when suddenly someone caught him. When he looked behind him, no one was there. This message resonated in a deep part of my being. It was similar to the feeling I got from reading Norman Vincent Peale. As I drove home that night, I called my mother to describe this experience to her. As we were talking, I unconsciously pulled my car into my local bar. Before I knew it, I was five beers deep. How the f*ck did I get here again?

Nothing seemed to matter anymore. My nose refused to let me snort cocaine without blood gushing out. I had a few possessions left in my room and a cockroach or two to keep me company. The small pink bureau I had pulled from the trash was now full of empty cocaine bags and cards for cutting lines. My dealer was now making day deliveries to my apartment so I could feel normal again, but I didn't care anymore. My bank accounts were in the negative, and I was going to die in Florida.

I was too ashamed to go home for Thanksgiving. Justin's wife, Julie, told me I could spend Thanksgiving with her Auntie Paula and Uncle Frank, who lived in an RV park at Disney World. I spent Thanksgiving eating turkey outside of an RV home. I was so grateful for Frank and Paula's kindness. The two of them had no idea the mess I was in, but their warm company brought me peace and happiness.

A few weeks after Thanksgiving, I started using cocaine early in the day and ingesting every drug I could find. When I arrived home that evening, I was highly intoxicated. My heart felt like it was beating out of my chest. I went to bed to try to calm myself down, but I began hallucinating. The hallucinations grew worse and worse. I started to believe it was the end. Instead of calling 911, I called the hospital and asked what the heart rate of a normal person was. I wasn't going to give up my addiction yet, even if it meant dying. I tried to time my heartbeats with my phone, but it became too difficult. The blackness grew deeper. I shut my phone off. I was ready.

After eight to ten hours of this experience, I was still alive. I turned my phone on to a barrage of messages. One from my employer, one from my roommate, and one from my brother. I knew the gig was up. I called Justin to tell him what was going on without mentioning the full severity of the situation. I visited my employer Mark to tell him I needed to go home to get help. I think he knew this day was coming. Mark asked me to do him a favor and join a men's group when I got back to New Hampshire. I promised him I would.

My plan was to leave Florida the next day, but I had no money to drive back to New Hampshire. Justin offered to send money. I picked up money from Western Union in the afternoon and headed home. I decided to stop at the bar since it was still early. The problem was that every time I drank, I wanted to use cocaine. After a few drinks, I called my dealer. Before I knew it, I had spent all of the money Justin sent me on cocaine.

The next morning, my feeling of horror was intense. How was I going to explain this to my brother? It took me the entire day to gather the courage to reach out to him. I parked my car at Arby's and hit the send button.

"Justin, I spent the money you sent me on cocaine."

"Are you serious?"

"Yeah, I don't know what to say."

"Listen, I'm going to send you money one more time," Justin said, "but if you spend it on cocaine, I'm writing you off!"

Those last four words saved my life. If I couldn't depend on my brother, I was done. He was my last glimmer of hope.

CHAPTER 3

THE NIGHTMARE BEFORE CHRISTMAS

The next day I went to pick up the money at Western Union. I could not mess up again. When I got home, I told Mike that he could not let me leave the house, even if he had to tackle me. I made it through the day sober. The next morning, I hugged Mike and began the twenty-three-hour drive back to New Hampshire. I moved to Florida to turn my life around from the hell of opioid addiction. Now I couldn't wait to leave this hot hellhole of death.

When I got to Georgia, I stopped at the first store I could find. I had lived in Florida for eight months and never purchased a single orange. It was supposed to be the orange mecca of the world! There's no way I was leaving without a Florida orange, even if it was bought in Georgia. When I put the oranges in the backseat, I noticed a small baggie of cocaine. I couldn't believe it. My mind raced with thoughts as I debated back and forth with myself about what to do with it. I knew it wasn't enough to get me high, so I knew one bag would turn into two. I got out of the car and threw it into the waste barrel.

I made it all the way to New Jersey before having an emotional and physical breakdown. Since I couldn't afford a hotel, my brother paid for a room. I could barely walk to the front counter due to my mental fog and exhaustion. As soon as I got to my room, I passed out. I finished the drive back to my mother's trailer in New Hampshire the next day. My mother had no idea what had happened in Florida. She had balloons and a cake awaiting my arrival. I asked my brother to promise me he wouldn't tell her what had happened. I failed to mention to him how serious my addiction really was. He made me promise him I wouldn't drink or use drugs for thirty days. I agreed with him.

Within three days, I was at a bar with a friend. He ordered a beer, and I ordered a soda. I told him what had happened in Florida. We decided to leave the bar and head back to his place. On his table was a plate with lines of cocaine on it. I started to sweat, and my throat got dry. I waited for him to offer me some, even after spending the last hour telling him I was back from Florida because of problems with cocaine. He apologized for having the cocaine and finished all the lines himself. Now I was pissed. I asked him if he could get me Percocet. I was only on day three of my thirty-day agreement, and I was getting high again.

I was dead broke and in debt. I drove to my old employer for a job selling phones again. My previous boss had yet to hear about what had happened in Florida. There was one position available at a newer location. I told them I would take it. When I walked outside the store, my cell phone began to ring. It was Mike. He was panicking. He told me federal agents were at the apartment looking for me, and he was worried he would go to jail. I told him I wasn't sure why they would be looking for me and hung up the phone.

A few minutes later, my phone rang again. This time it was a familiar voice. It was the same agent who arrested me eight months earlier. He said they had an arrest warrant, and I was going to be arraigned in federal court in a few days.

What happened next was a blur. Even though I was a day or two sober, I had a blackout. A sober blackout! I ended up driving for an hour without knowing where I was. What was I going to tell my family? The past had finally caught up with me, and I knew I was going away for a long time.

The day had finally arrived. I was now being held in a jail cell in a federal courthouse. After a few hours in the cell, the doors opened, and a young man wearing an orange jumpsuit entered. We didn't say a word to each other until the guards served us food and a drink. I felt comfortable enough to talk when the caffeine kicked in. When I asked him what he was in for, he told me he got caught with possession of Oxycontin and was doing time for it. I swallowed hard. Not only had they arrested me with dozens of pills, there was that other package I never received. I started to see my future through the lens of this young man.

I was soon brought before my court-appointed lawyer, Jon. He asked me what my crime was, and when I told him, his exact words were, "Take this whole thing with a grain of salt." He didn't seem to be taking it seriously. I was walked into the federal courtroom, handcuffed at my ankles and my wrists. I glanced over to my right to see my mother, brother, and his wife, all crying. They were told I was looking at seven-plus years in a federal prison. The judge and prosecutor proceeded with the discovery report. I pleaded no contest and walked out of the courtroom. They didn't set bail, so I was free to be with my family for Christmas.

It was the quietest Christmas I can remember. We ordered Chinese food, and as I sat eating my beef teriyaki, I thought to myself, Am I going to spend the next seven years of my life in federal prison? What would this do to my family? I grabbed a fortune cookie and broke it open. The fortune cookie read, "God will help you overcome any hardship." I told my mother and brother what it said. Despite my adversities, there was still hope. I held onto this message tightly. I knew I would have to attain unwavering faith and resilience if I was going to stay sober and do the next right thing every day. I didn't realize it at the time, but I was beginning to develop a strong why for my life, and I knew I didn't want to spend my twenties in federal prison.

I BEGAN TO SENSE THIS WHOLE SITUATION MIGHT HAVE A GREATER PURPOSE.

On New Year's Day, I got the message to go for my first urinalysis, but the building was closed. I freaked out because I knew a probation violation meant prison time. As it turned out, they were closed for the holiday. I was required to check in each day to get a urinalysis. When I met my pretrial probation officer, Jodi, she handed me a few papers to be signed at Alcoholics Anonymous (AA) and Narcotics Anonymous (NA) meetings. I was required to attend these groups weekly. At my first AA meeting, I could barely get out of my car I was so nervous. Once inside, I heard a man named Skip share his experience, strength, and hope. I took the job of making coffee at my first meeting. My recovery plan for alcohol and substance abuse treatment from the court was to avoid using drugs and alcohol, work full time, go to meetings, and see a therapist.

The court provided a drug and alcohol counselor named Bonnie Halsey. In our first session together, I was very emotional. I broke down crying and told her about the time I had to call 911 as a kid when I found my mom not breathing. I told her about my addictions and my father leaving when I was four. I told her about the lines I promised myself I would never cross, but that I had eventually crossed them all. She must have thought I was falling apart. But getting all that stuff off my chest made me feel a little better.

Bonnie was one of the first people on my recovery support team. She was the first person with whom I felt safe sharing anything on my mind, knowing she'd receive it without judgment. I know many people could benefit from having a Bonnie in their life. Bonnie was an angel. She helped me work through many traumas and issues unrelated to drugs and alcohol as well. If you're struggling with mental health conditions and/or addiction to drugs, alcohol, pornography, and so forth, I strongly recommend seeking out professional help.

Every Sunday, I attended church with my mother. Her strong commitment to her faith planted important seeds in my early recovery. She introduced me to my first mentor in recovery named Pastor Robert Baily. Pastor Bob had a connection with Norman Vincent Peale and even had the chance to spend time with him. I met with Pastor Bob on a weekly basis to talk about my life. He referred to passages in the Bible to help me with whatever topic I brought up. He suggested I pray every morning and night. He was a close friend and mentor for several years.

In the first few weeks of recovery, Pastor Bob suggested I journal every day. I purchased my first journal and began writing down what I was grateful for. I would write, "I'm grateful to have a job and provide a service to my customers," and "I'm grateful for my family." I would write out things that happened during the day, especially when things didn't go my way. For example, in my first month in recovery, a customer got very upset with me about his bill. His anger triggered my suppressed feelings of anger, and I reacted very poorly. I lacked the coping tools to deal with my new feelings and emotions. I was fortunate to still have a job after that outburst.

Pastor Bob told me about a group of men called the Wednesday Warriors. I remembered the promise I had made to Mark in Florida about joining a men's group. The group met every Wednesday at 6:30 a.m., rain or shine. I hated getting up early, but I did it anyway. The men in this group prayed over me more times than I can count. I had struggled to trust older men my entire life since my dad had left. Now I had a group of men graciously praying over me for the upcoming trial I was facing. I shed many tears in front of these men, and I owe a huge debt of gratitude to each one of them.

I kept in regular contact with my court-appointed lawyer Jon. He told me the prosecutor wanted to put me away. But I was doing the next right thing every day: attending 12-Step meetings, attending a men's group, seeing a therapist, working full time, taking a class at a community college, practicing new habits, and doing service work. Despite my panic attacks, I was doing good for myself.

After a few months, I got a call from Jon. The prosecution made an offer for me to spend eleven months in federal prison. I told Jon I was not going to accept this offer, and I wanted to meet the prosecutor. I told him I wanted to share my story with him directly, so he would know where I was coming from. He told me this was a bad idea since he knew the prosecutor. Despite my warnings, the date was set. In the past I would have listened to Jon, but this time I decided to trust my intuition. During the meeting with the prosecutor, I shared some of my story, but the prosecutor kept emphasizing I was a criminal. Afterwards, I told Jon I was very concerned. Once again, he said his famous last words, "Take what he said with a grain of salt."

A short time later, I got an urgent message to meet Jon. He sat me down and told me I was not going to spend time in prison. This was a special moment for my family. I was grateful I had listened to my intuition. On January 4, 2007, I was back in a federal courtroom for my hearing. Jon asked if I wanted to say any words to the judge. I told him I wanted to advocate for my recovery and show my family the man I was becoming. I shared with the court that I was over a year in recovery, going back to school, and working a strong recovery program. I expected the judge to tell me how great I was doing. Instead, the judge told me he was happy for my recovery, but if I ever stepped foot in his courtroom again, I would be doing all of my time. Reality check! However, the judge gave me a second chance. I know many of us never get a second chance. I never got to personally thank him, but over a decade later I met a father who lost his son to a drug overdose. He heard my story and said he was a lawyer who knew how to contact the judge. He was able to send my thank you message to the judge for his decision to keep me out of prison over a decade earlier.

Here's the message I received from my lawyer friend:

I called the U.S. District Court in New Hampshire and spoke today with [name], the judge before whom you appeared over a decade ago.

I told [the judge] the amazing things you are doing and how you have committed your life to helping people struggling with addiction.

I related that you had told me that none of this would have been possible had [he] sent you to jail rather than giving you a second chance at life through probation.

I said that you had wanted to thank him, but did not know how to contact him, or whether contact was permitted (I am informed that direct contact with the sentencing judge is not permitted.)

[The judge] said your thank you made his day ... then he said it made his week!

When I look back at the progress I made in early recovery, it all started with my daily practices and connection. My daily routine helped me stay focused on my recovery and take drastic action. My connections with my recovery team provided support and accountability. As my new life continued, these daily practices became the foundation stone.

CHAPTER 4

THE FEARS RECOVERY TOOLKIT

When we choose to take responsibility for our life on a daily basis, we are faced with many challenges. This can be intimidating in early recovery. I was over $19,000 in debt, my car had been repossessed, and I had a panic disorder. Not only did I need to learn how to manage my stress, I had to figure out how to pay my bills on time, rebuild my credit, go to the grocery store, cook ... the list went on and on.

What got me through the first few years was my dedication to daily practices. I focused on my recovery, created a recovery team, read, talked to mentors, journaled, repeated affirmations, followed my intuition, and practiced self-care. I continued practicing each tool until it became a habit. Whenever I stopped doing my daily practices, my life became overwhelming.

For eight years, I worked at the same job and stayed consistent with my recovery toolkit. I had thought about leaving and trying something different, but fear kept me in my comfort zone. That all changed the day I decided to purchase my first house. The only house I had ever lived in was sold because of my father's addiction. For the next decade, my family had moved from one location to the next. When my realtor began sending me listings for homes in the city that I'd found recovery in, I was determined to make my dream a reality. It was the same town where I worked, found friends in recovery, and was arraigned in federal court. I figured keeping things local was a good reminder of how far I'd come.

After months of searching, I found a home that seemed inexpensive for what it offered. It had a sizeable driveway with four bedrooms. As soon as I pulled into the driveway, I knew it was the one. The home was in foreclosure and needed significant work before I could move in. I made an offer and waited. After a little negotiating, the offer was accepted.

I avoided leaving my job because it was familiar and safe. Every time I considered looking for a new job, fear would creep in. If I ventured into the job marketplace, I knew I would have to tell my new employer I was a felon. But the pressure and stress of paying bills left me little choice. It was time to get out of my comfort zone and find a higher paying position.

The most obvious choice was to work for Verizon Wireless Corporate. Verizon's online application included a question about previous arrests. I knew honesty was everything, so I put down as much detail as I thought was necessary. I was doubtful I was going to hear back since I had not one but two federal felonies.

A few weeks later, I was notified of my first phone interview. I was stunned. A person from human resources called and asked me questions based on my application. Eventually she got to the section about my felony charges. I told her about my past struggles with addiction and my problem with cocaine, alcohol, and Oxycontin, and how I got the federal charges as a result. I also told her about my recovery. I told her I was now eight years in recovery, working a strong program, and had just graduated with my undergraduate degree in psychology. I mentioned every detail to the point she probably felt uncomfortable. I figured if Verizon was going to hire me, I would have nothing to hide! I was confident I would be one of their top employees. I just needed them to give me a chance. When the call ended, I felt peace come into my heart. I knew that if they gave me another interview after that amount of honesty, I would get the job.

A week later I was notified of a second phone interview. I was overwhelmed by feelings of gratitude and joy. My second interview was similar to the first. They proceeded to ask about my charges, and once again I told them everything.

They informed me I made it to a final in-person interview. My in-person interview was very short, and I did not feel great about it. After weeks of not hearing anything, I figured I should start negotiating higher pay with my current employer. Suddenly a strong thought came in: No! You've come too far to give up now. If they were concerned about you being a felon, why were there additional interviews? I immediately called human resources and asked if they had heard about the decision. To my disappointment, they told me I did not get the job.

A week later, they called me back about another chance to interview. I knew I had to bring out the best version of myself. During the interview, I asked the manager to challenge my sales and negotiation skills on the sales floor. She was taken by surprise but accepted my challenge. A few days later, they called and told me I got the job. Tears streamed down my face. In that moment, I had a deep appreciation for my recovery. I would no longer allow my mind or people's opinions to keep me living in fear.

I promised myself I would use fear as a compass to lead me to what I needed to do next.

For the next two years, I won several sales awards and doubled my income. I was now in my early thirties and traveling the world for the first time. I continued my education by enrolling in a master's program in clinical mental health counseling. This decision brought tremendous fear and doubt. How can I afford it? How will I be able to handle the course load and work full time? I'm not smart enough for this. Despite feelings of self-doubt and insecurity, I charged forward. I figured fear and doubt would always be there, but I could choose to have the courage to do what was right, not what was easy and comfortable.

That's when I learned that facing fear can lead us to our higher purpose. For example, one of my biggest stressors was my social anxiety. Despite being very successful in sales, I spent most of my time after work alone. I labeled myself an introvert. I worried the panic attacks I suffered in the first five years of recovery would return. I lived with social anxiety for so long that I believed it would be there for the rest of my life. On many occasions, I could not leave my house to go food shopping because I was overwhelmed with severe anxiety. Despite nine years of recovery from drug and alcohol addiction, I was still in bondage to anxiety. It often happened at work. One of the methods that helped was to lock myself in the bathroom, place paper towels on the floor, and get on my knees to take a few deep breaths and pray.

I took anxiety medication for many years of my recovery, but I decided it was now time to see Bonnie again. I told her I was going to stop the medication and start meeting regularly with her. I'm not recommending anyone get off their medication and follow my path. My goal was to overcome my anxiety. I began reading several books on shyness and overcoming social anxiety. I started using cognitive behavioral therapy, dialectical behavioral therapy, acceptance and commitment therapy, and emotional freedom technique, also known as tapping. Every day I wrote down my thoughts in my anxiety journal and the situations that triggered my anxiety, including my physical symptoms like increased heart rate, bodily discomfort, sweaty palms, trouble thinking clearly, and feelings of doom.

Here's an entry from my anxiety journal:

11/20/2014 Thursday: I did not drive to Chipotle on Amherst St. I had fear and felt anxiety about people thinking I am going to do something or be looked at as weird.

I also wrote down experiments, such as talking to one stranger a day, inviting someone out to coffee, smiling at one stranger a day, and initiating a conversation everywhere I went. I honestly hated doing this. Most weeks, I would only perform a few of these actions. I convinced myself I was a great mind reader because I assumed people were thinking and talking about me all of the time. These thoughts are not abnormal when you have severe anxiety. I determined people were unfriendly, insensitive, and even hostile without ever saying a word to them. I wrote in my journal, "Do I really know what people are thinking?" Maybe people were not actually judging, evaluating, or even thinking of me. Maybe they were doing the best they could like I was. Maybe my own thoughts and belief systems were causing my pain and anxiety. As I continued with these mini experiments, I noticed people were not as scary as I thought.

My manager Jenn offered a helpful suggestion. "Whenever you speak to a group of people," she said, "look for the person in the group you have inspired most." I started to use this technique whenever I was required to speak to a group of coworkers or at a meeting. It worked amazingly well and reduced my anxiety.

Using more appreciative self-talk also helped. Before each sale, I began to say to myself, "I'm the best salesman in New Hampshire." This might sound arrogant, but it worked. I went on to become the top salesman in New Hampshire. Shyness became a strength instead of a weakness. I would ask myself, "What's great about being shy?" I would repeat the affirmation, "My shyness and time alone have taught me how to be a loving, kind, and compassionate human being." I started to accept the fact I was just a highly sensitive person. I really enjoyed being a deep listener. Being highly sensitive was a superpower with customers because it created genuine conversations.

Mindfulness and meditation were also helpful tools for anxiety. I wish I had started practicing these earlier! I started with a six-minute silent meditation with my eyes closed, where I paid attention to the sounds happening around me. Guided meditations were also helpful. My day was noticeably different when I meditated versus days I did not. (We will dive deeper into mindfulness and meditation techniques in Chapter 9: Self-Care in Recovery.)

Caffeine use is highly accepted in recovery. It helped me get through work in the morning and overcome the afternoon slump at 3:00 p.m. I used it before social interactions and speaking obligations. Pre-workout drinks before going to the gym were also a must. For seven years, I drank two Red Bulls a day and always kept a case in my trunk. The day came when I had to face the truth: caffeine was contributing to my anxiety. But how was I going to cope without my daily dose? Caffeine had become a best friend that got me through countless speaking engagements and social interactions I often dreaded.

If I could stop using heroin, cocaine, painkillers, and alcohol, caffeine should be easy to quit, right?

A friend of mine, Nick Wright, recommended I try taking cold showers for thirty days. Nick was someone who always offered helpful ideas. Because it was wintertime in New Hampshire, I didn't take him seriously. But when my roommate decided to take a cold shower, I had to do it. My first cold shower was painful. I turned the shower dial all the way cold (big mistake), turned on some music, and jumped in. The water was so cold it took my breath away for what felt like sixty seconds. I stayed in the cold water for a full five minutes. When I came out, my face and body were red. I headed out to a meeting an hour or so later. When I walked into the meeting, something was different. My normal feelings of anxiousness around people were gone. The only thing I had done differently that evening was a cold shower. This intrigued me so much that I continued the thirty-day challenge.

About five months later, I experienced a terrible panic attack after drinking a sugar-free Red Bull. This incident brought about a huge wave of fear, and I knew I had to make a change. My first small step was to stop buying cases of Red Bull. Then, instead of drinking two Red Bulls a day, I switched to one. I then switched to drinking coffee and black tea for a few weeks. When I got down to drinking black tea a few times a day, I made the decision to quit caffeine for good on my first trip to the West Coast.

During my first day in California, I drank only green tea. This trip was incredibly uplifting to my spirit, as we visited meditation gardens and walked along the beautiful coastline of Encinitas. By the last day of our trip, I stopped drinking caffeine altogether. That first day without caffeine was a rough one. I came down with severe cold- and flu-like symptoms. Surprisingly, the next day I felt much better. It took one day of severe withdrawal to kick an addiction I'd had for ten years. Today, my energy levels have never been higher. I've had a significant decrease in anxiety and no panic attacks for the last five years.

WHAT WE FEAR THE MOST IS OFTEN WHAT WE NEED TO FACE THE MOST.

If you want to reach your full potential, you'll need to find the courage to walk through fear. I'm going to help you with this in part two of this book. I heard a speaker once share, "If you're not scared, you're not playing big enough." The more I walk outside my comfort zone, the more I encounter fear—and the more I grow.

By this point, my daily recovery toolkit had solidified into five essential practices:

1. **Focus on my recovery.** Every day, I will put my recovery first. My priorities are going to recovery meetings, focusing on my purpose, and reminding myself why I choose recovery. Focusing on my recovery means focusing on my connections—staying in daily contact with at least one person on my recovery team. These connections are critical. I never have to do this recovery journey alone.

2. **Elevate my recovery.** I will read books, listen to audios, attend events, and watch documentaries about ways to elevate my recovery. I will follow the vision I create for my life. I will practice visualization and post my intentions and goals where I can see them. I will learn from mentors and role models.

3. **Appreciate my recovery.** Every day I will journal my gratitude and any new ideas I discover. I will repeat affirmations and choose my words carefully. I appreciate the power of my recovery story and will not be ashamed of my past. I will encourage people to share their stories of recovery, and I will be of service to others.

4. **Resilience in recovery.** I will continue building a resilient mind and heart. I will face my fears and take actions outside of my comfort zone. I will trust my intuition on a daily basis and write down the times I notice meaningful coincidences or synchronicities.

5. **Self-care in recovery.** I will follow my own self-care routine. I will practice movement every day and be in nature as often as possible. I will make sleep a priority and nourish myself with healthy foods that provide energy, while avoiding foods that drain energy. I will pay closer attention to my sensitivities and heal my past trauma. I will practice mindfulness on a daily basis.

> *You will never change your life*
> *until you change something you do daily.*
> *The secret of your success is found in your daily routine.*
>
> John Maxwell

What about you? Where are you on your road to recovery? When I was getting high, obtaining my next fix was nonnegotiable. Today my daily practices are nonnegotiable.

When we begin recovery, we need a plan. Whether you're struggling to get two days in a row, or you've been in recovery for years, you can benefit from the recovery toolkit in part two. My friend Snook has offered to share his story—not to draw attention to me, but to plant seeds for what is possible in your life.

Snook's Story

My nickname growing up was the Red Rooster. I had bright red hair and an incredible amount of energy. When I eventually began drinking and using drugs, I would be the last one awake at parties and hollering at 5:00 a.m., waking everybody up. Partying became my life. I had finally found the missing puzzle piece, the solution to my equation. The glory days began fading very quickly for me in my party career, however. Countless arrests, constant blackouts, and many apologies became tightly intertwined into my story. The police arrested me on five separate occasions for drunk driving, and I was even kicked out of the United States Navy for my uncontrollably chaotic behavior. That is not an easy thing to do.

The rooster days were over. Back home, I continued partying as if nothing had happened. Now I could finally drink the way I wanted. The way I wanted looked like me continuing to burn bridge after bridge and become more and more isolated. I went in and out of jails and psychiatric wards, with nobody coming to visit me except my mom. I knew something needed to change, but I didn't know what until somebody in the recovery unit on G-block of Rockingham County Correctional Facility told me that I didn't have to live like that anymore.

Sobriety was weird, but I held on and great things began to happen. I received my driver's license back and bought a brand-new car. A healthy community began building up around me. I was now five years sober with a master's degree and had a great job. All these incredible things began happening in my life, but something was still missing. Why was I so empty inside?

Inevitably I relapsed into alcohol and drug use, which brought me right back to the jails and psychiatric wards. I handed away my brand-new car, my apartment, my employment, my relationships, and worst of all, any bit of self-respect that I had left over from those five great years of sobriety. But I had a master's degree in social work; what the heck went wrong? It was time to give the recovery thing another shot. There had to be more to sobriety than getting a nine-to-five job and rejoining mainstream society.

Months later, I was a few months sober again, and that's when I met Jesse for the first time. I was once again living in a homeless shelter for veterans in Nashua. We began working together to help me stay sober by attending meetings and writing out an extensive personal inventory on my life. I would hop into his car with an energy drink in one hand and a lit cigarette in the other, claiming how healthy I was becoming by crushing weights at the gym for five hours a day. Jesse would consistently receive my ramblings about how a relationship was crumbling and how I would like him to fix it for me. He would just smirk, and we would continue on with the work. This lasted a couple of years, all the while he was planting subtle little seeds of wisdom.

Those seeds eventually began blossoming. I thought Jesse was just going to help me with getting sober again, but what he ended up helping me find was much larger than I could have ever imagined. Jesse helped me immensely by showing me the power of manifesting. A few years into my new recovery, I was dating a girl and we became pregnant. I expressed to Jesse that I should start looking into buying a house but did not know where to start. Jesse gladly accepted my cry for help, and the very first thing he had me do was write out a goal card that consisted of the goal, why I desired this goal, when I wanted it completed by, the steps to take, and how this achievement was going to benefit my life. I was slightly skeptical at first, but I began looking at this goal card by my bedside table every morning. Not only did I reach my desired goal, but I completed it in less than half the time.

Jesse also began teaching me the art of visualization. I created an intention board on his recommendation that I reviewed every day. He showed me how to turn my disgusting eating habits into healthy ways to nourish my body. Jesse gave me a method of journaling that was powered directly through my heart. With all these new tools he taught me, I began writing my own book and have made preparations to branch out into my own private practice in order to help people the way I have been helped. Practicing these new techniques opened an infinite number of possibilities and helped me achieve the feeling of fulfillment I was seeking. Now, I cannot wait to see what else I can create!

In part two, I'm going to walk you through the FEARS recovery toolkit step by step. This framework is very practical, and each of the following chapters contain action steps for you to complete. I've designed each chapter to help you immediately put what you're learning into practice. If you do the work, the results will be rewarding. You're worthy of greatness.

Are you ready to start?

PART TWO:

OVERCOME FEAR WITH FEARS

CHAPTER 5

FOCUS ON YOUR RECOVERY

*Where you place your attention
is where you place your energy.*

Dr. Joe Dispenza

The first part of the FEARS recovery toolkit is to *focus on your recovery*. This means making your recovery priority number one, no matter what. Focusing on your recovery is the most important aspect of this book. If we don't place our focus and attention on recovery, we will eventually lose it.

The beautiful thing about recovery is it looks different for every person. What works in one season of life may not work as well in a different season of life. Discovering what works best will be an important part of the journey. What's essential is to create a recovery program of *action*. Focusing on your recovery might involve attending a self-help group, attending 12-Step meetings, a daily yoga practice, mindfulness meditation, writing, creating art or music, a religious ceremony, exercising, or being in nature. Being connected to a community of people in recovery is also helpful. I will highlight what's worked well for myself and the people I've learned from. No matter what path you take, when you focus on your recovery every day, you will be successful. You will create a life you love waking up to. I've witnessed this fact time and time again.

If our first step is to focus on our recovery, what *is* recovery exactly? The Substance Abuse and Mental Health Services Administration (SAMHSA) defines recovery as "a process of change in which individuals improve their health and wellness, live a self-directed life, and strive to reach their full potential." I think this definition is useful. When you choose to focus on your recovery, you are choosing to improve your health and wellness, you are choosing to reach your full potential, and you are choosing to live a self-directed life. Ultimately the actions you choose to take (or not to take) determine whether or not you reach your highest potential in life. Choosing to focus on your recovery will become a habit and a lifestyle.

CREATE A DAILY TO-DO LIST

When I was in active addiction, my primary focus was to get rid of the pain and my uncomfortable feelings by reaching for something outside of myself. My addiction numbed out any feelings of discontent, discomfort, and separation, but the consequences of my actions led to anxiety, shame, and guilt—leading to more pain, and more numbing.

To break this vicious cycle, I had to shift my focus to recovery, which meant asking for help, being willing to listen, and taking radical action. It also meant avoiding people, environments, and situations that put my recovery in jeopardy. One of the first tools I used to focus on my recovery was *a daily to-do list.*

Your first step is to write down your recovery actions in a daily planner. In early recovery, some of the actions I wrote down were "attend a meeting," "exercise," "see Bonnie," "talk to my sponsor or mentor," and "connect with Jay" (part of my recovery team). Your next step is to write down other priorities like family, work, and school. My point is that recovery actions come *first.* If you don't write it down, it's not a priority. Writing down a daily routine gives you clarity, peace of mind, and a sense of purpose.[8] Fifteen years later, I still write down my recovery actions on a daily to-do list.

> **Action Step:**
>
> Buy yourself a daily planner or use a calendar app on your smartphone to record your recovery actions each day. Recovery actions can include attending a self-help group, meditation, exercise, and service to others—whatever will support you in your recovery. Next, write down your other priorities and plans for the day. Keep a daily to-do list every day for the next 30 days.

BUILD YOUR RECOVERY TEAM

Being able to feel safe with other people is probably the single most important aspect of mental health.

Bessel van der Kolk, MD

Our connections matter. You do not have to do this recovery journey alone. Your next step is to *build a recovery team.* Your recovery team will consist of people who support you with no strings attached. Your recovery team might include a sponsor, a mentor, a friend, a family member, a spiritual advisor, a therapist, a doctor, or a recovery coach. Your recovery team will provide valuable feedback and keep you accountable. My first-year recovery team consisted of my mother, brother, mentor, therapist, recovery sponsor, and probation officer. These were the people in my life who reminded me that recovery comes first. Today, my recovery team consists of five recovery friends I connect with consistently.

Since connection is the opposite of addiction, I recommend building your recovery team as soon as possible. Your recovery experience will bring many highs and many lows. When we experience moments of depression, anxiety, pain, guilt, panic, fear, or shame, we need a person who will be there to listen. We can ask for help by connecting with our recovery team. We are all recovering from something, so creating a recovery team is for everyone. If you don't resonate with the term *recovery team*, simply change the name to support team, dream team, recovery tribe, sober support team, recovery warriors, or whatever name works for you. Your recovery team members will change and update as you evolve and grow. Remember, this is a group of people who support your recovery 100 percent, accept the authentic you, are good for your mental health, and show compassion towards your recovery journey. Your recovery team will call you out on your shit from time to time. If they don't meet these conditions, they are not fit for your recovery team.

Who are the people in your life today who could be on your recovery team?

Action Step:

Write down 3–5 people you will ask to be on your recovery team. These are individuals who believe in your recovery and will keep you accountable. If you can't think of 3–5 people, name at least 1 person.

My Recovery Team:

1.

2.

3.

4.

5.

Great job! This is your recovery team: people with whom you feel safe sharing your struggles, cravings, challenges, emotions, ideas, and thoughts. Connect with your recovery team on a daily basis. Your recovery team will be managed and nurtured by you.

Action Step:

Reach out to your new recovery team in the next 24 hours and let them know you're grateful to have them in your corner.

If you don't have anyone to add to your recovery team, write down the actions you will take in the next 24 hours to build your recovery team. Who will you reach out to?

Building a recovery team is a matter of life and death for many people. We *need* connection to people we can count on when things don't go our way, especially early in recovery.

If you still can't think of anyone, call a recovery hotline, go to intherooms.com, or type "recovery meetings, AA meetings, ACA meetings, NA meetings, HA meetings, CA meetings, GA meetings, SA meetings, FA meetings, OA meetings, DA meetings, SMART Recovery, Celebrate Recovery, or Al-Anon meetings" into Google to find the appropriate group in your area. Members of your recovery team do not need to be your friends. It could include someone you met at a recovery meeting or a trained professional who supports you. I know asking for help is hard at first, but it will save your life. We think we are alone in the world, but there is always someone who can hold a safe space for you.

KEEP YOURSELF ACCOUNTABLE IN RECOVERY

Accountability in recovery is indispensable. When I was in active addiction, I wasn't accountable to anyone and my recklessness caught up with me. Your new recovery team is who will hold you accountable. In my first year of recovery, I stayed accountable to my probation officer, mother, sponsor, and brother at least once a day. I eventually found a recovery sponsor at a 12-Step meeting and a mentor I could be accountable to. Today I stay accountable to my recovery team by keeping in constant contact. This means a minimum of one text message a day to at least one member of my recovery team. When you focus on your recovery, you attract people into your life who want to emulate your success. People will trust that you will keep them accountable to their own recovery journey. I receive a text message check-in from people in recovery every day, some with thirty-plus years of recovery and others new to the recovery journey. These individuals also keep me accountable to my recovery.

> **Action Step:**
>
> Ask your recovery team for permission to check in with them on a daily basis as needed. Send a text or call at least one person on your recovery team every day. Schedule a time to meet with them weekly, even if it's virtually on Zoom. Please don't take this step lightly. Many of us have lost friends and family who didn't know they could ask for help.

Accountability is especially helpful for behavioral addictions. Due to our highly sexualized society and easy accessibility, internet pornography seems normal today. Internet pornography is known as "supernormal stimuli," meaning it can take over our normal instincts in return for large blasts of dopamine.[9] While serious shame and stigma still exist with drug and alcohol addiction, the stigma around internet pornography is often much worse. More and more men and women struggle with this silent epidemic. If you struggle with internet pornography and sex addiction, I recommend asking for help by finding people to stay accountable to. You can try finding a recovery support group online or in person, read the book *Your Brain on Porn* to learn about cognitive neuroscience and first-person accounts, and seek out professional help.[10] Despite failing many times with internet pornography, I never gave up. Like most addictions, it's one day at a time. When the pain became great enough, I asked for help. I now have people on my recovery team to whom I stay accountable regarding internet pornography.

WHAT HAPPENS IF I DON'T FOCUS ON MY RECOVERY?

In my second year of recovery, I got into a serious relationship. This relationship quickly became more important than focusing on my recovery. It wasn't long before my life started to unravel, and I stopped reaching out to my recovery team. I started to hurt the people I loved with my attitude, actions, and behaviors. Once again, when the mental, emotional, physical, and spiritual pain was great enough, I ended the relationship and began focusing on my recovery.

Pain is one of the greatest motivators for change. The lesson I learned is whatever you put in front of your recovery will be lost.

FINDING PURPOSE IN RECOVERY

What is purpose? Purpose can be a direction, goal, or reason for living in recovery. My purpose in early recovery was to refrain from using drugs and alcohol, work hard at my job, and do the next right thing every day. I made coffee at 12-Step meetings, greeted people, and made commitments to share my story with others. But over time, I felt stuck and yearned for something more. I should just be grateful for being in recovery and having a job, right? The truth was I needed a bigger *why*. Why did I choose recovery in the first place? Getting clear on this question helped direct my actions and goals.

> # LIVING ON PURPOSE HELPS YOU FOCUS ON YOUR RECOVERY BECAUSE IT ACTIVATES A POWERFUL REASON TO STAY ON THE PATH.

It may seem too early to talk about big topics like knowing your purpose in early recovery. "I don't even have a place to stay right now," you may be thinking. "How can I think about my life purpose?" But I'm here to show that you can *start* with purpose. Your purpose doesn't have to be some big existential idea. It can be as simple as, "My purpose is to focus on my recovery." "My purpose is to provide for my daughter." "My purpose is to take care of my health and wellness."

Recovery allows us to create a self-directed life of our own choosing. If we choose not to live on purpose, we are settling for less than what we are capable of. When I ask people in recovery if they have a purpose, they usually tell me yes. But they're not always sure what it is or how to achieve it. I will share with them that purpose begins with clarity, guidance, and following your heart. Our adversities can help us discover our purpose. People also find their purpose in creating art, music, dance, poetry, books, and speaking to groups of people. For some, living on purpose is being a loving and supportive father, mother, child or sibling, connecting to a power greater than themselves, or becoming a recovery coach.

Bronnie Ware, author of *Top Five Regrets of the Dying*, wrote a remarkable memoir about working at the bedside of those in hospice care. Bronnie learned that as people see their lives coming to an end, their most common regret by far is that they never had the courage to live their own lives, and instead lived the lives that people around them expected.[11] Recovery offers us a tremendous second chance to live our own lives. You can start your life over and live on purpose every single day. If your purpose is simply to stay in recovery, that's great. Just remember you are on this earth for a reason, and recovery will help you find that reason.

Working with people in addiction and mental health recovery is a central part of my purpose. Bill Wilson states, "Helping others is the foundation stone of your recovery."[12] When I'm helping a person who struggles with what I once battled, I'm living my purpose. This is because service to others is the greatest act of love. Service to others includes helping family members, coworkers, neighbors, and our human family.

Action Step:

This is Jack Canfield's Life Purpose Exercise from his book *The Success Principles*.[13] I've found it to be useful in finding your purpose, and I've used this process with many people in recovery.

Follow the instructions to create your purpose statement:

1. List 2 of your unique personal qualities or strengths (such as enthusiasm, resilience, empathy, creativity, humor, organization).

2. List 2 ways you enjoy expressing each of those qualities and strengths when interacting with others (such as to support, to inspire, to create, to harmonize).

3. Now assume the world is perfect. What does this world look like? How is everyone interacting with everyone else? What does it feel like? Write your answer as a statement, in the present tense, describing the ultimate condition, the perfect world as you see it and feel it. Remember, a perfect world is a fun place to be! (For example: Everyone is freely expressing their own unique talents. Everyone is working in harmony. Everyone is in unity and expressing love.)

4. Now combine each of the previous 3 elements to write a single statement. For example: My purpose is to use my creativity and enthusiasm to support and inspire others to freely express their talents in a harmonious and loving way.

Write your purpose statement here:

Here's my purpose statement: *My purpose is to use my passion, authenticity, and intuition to help others genuinely express their unique stories and strengths in a loving, powerful way.*

Your purpose statement can be short and sweet, such as "My purpose is to be compassionate, loving, and supportive to all those I encounter."

Once you've created your purpose statement, place it where you can read it every day. I wrote down my purpose statement every day until I could remember it. Write it on a 3 x 5 index card and carry it with you or tape it to your bathroom mirror.

Your purpose statement should energize you. Share your purpose statement with your recovery team. You can update or add to your purpose statement at any time.

Living on purpose shifts you from a mindset of scarcity to a mindset of abundance. Scarcity only exists in your mind. Abundance is all around you. The mainstream media constantly fills our heads with the idea that we live in scarcity. "Every man for himself!" But we live in an abundant universe. In fact, this is the most abundant time to be alive in human history, thanks to our technological advancements. When you live on purpose, you see opportunities that didn't exist before—not because those opportunities weren't there, but because your perception has changed. Our perception creates our reality. Living with purpose takes us out of the habit of comparison and competition with others. In active addiction, I would constantly compare myself to others and say things like "At least I'm not as bad as that person," or "That person's addiction is much worse than mine"—and continue justifying my destructive behaviors. Have you ever done this? Always focus on your *own* recovery and purpose.

Action Step:
Answer the following questions.
   Why is it important for me to focus on my recovery?

   What is it about recovery that gives me a deep sense of meaning, purpose, and fulfillment?

When are times I've been at my best, when I've fully come alive?

Why am I here?

Take 5 to 10 minutes to write your responses. Your answers to these questions will help you gain more clarity about your purpose in recovery.

Every day, ask yourself this question: What one thing can I do, no matter how small, that would help me focus on my recovery?

CHAPTER 6

ELEVATE YOUR RECOVERY

If you read good books every morning, visualize and strategize your goals, and write your insights in your journal, you'll have an amazing life.

Dr. Benjamin Hardy

Elevate your recovery is the second part of the FEARS recovery toolkit. In this chapter, you'll discover new ways to be creative, adventurous, and connected in recovery. Some ideas might be new to you because no one teaches you this stuff in school, college, or at your job. Elevating your recovery involves elevating your knowledge, elevating your circle, and elevating your vision. You'll learn about the importance of being a lifelong learner and surrounding yourself with mentors who continually learn, set goals, visualize, and talk to mentors of their own. I will also show you how to use visualization as a way to create intentions and goals for your recovery.

Before I found recovery, I would run, hide, or get high if a situation appeared hopeless. What I failed to understand is that every experience is here to teach you something. As the saying goes, if you want something you've never had before, you must do what you've never done before. Going back to the way things used to be is no longer an option. You don't have to wait until you have a steady income, your family back, or a stable life to start practicing these tools. You can start now. Let's dive into some of the ways you can elevate your recovery on a daily basis.

ELEVATE YOUR KNOWLEDGE

Earth is one big school. Some call it the school of hard knocks, but I like to call it the school of life. You can choose to learn whatever you desire using various means of acquiring knowledge. Reading is one essential tool that can advance your life. I recommend reading books that inspire you to move toward a purpose. The truth is that I don't remember most of what I read. What I do remember are the ideas or lessons I put into practice and experiment with. To expand your skills and capabilities, put what you're reading into practice right away. For example, when I wanted to learn how to read faster, I chose a book on speed-reading that provided tools and methods for me to try. The next time I picked up a book, I practiced one technique I learned at a time. I recommend you do the exact same thing with this book to avoid overwhelming yourself.

> **Action Step:**
> Read 5 pages out of a book every day for the next 30 days.

Another way to elevate your recovery is to learn by listening. When I'm in my car, going for a walk, or exercising, I usually listen to an audiobook, podcast, or YouTube video. My car is now a mobile center for learning, growth, and healing. I have felt anxious, angry, sad, or depressed in my car on a number of occasions. After listening to an inspiring audiobook or YouTube video for ten or fifteen minutes, I experience a higher vibration and calmer mood. I recommend listening to inspiring audiobooks more than once. For example, I've listened to Susan Jeffers's book *Feel the Fear and Do It Anyway* and Michael Singer's *The Untethered Soul* at least eight to ten times. I hear something new every time I listen.

If you want to elevate your recovery, cut back or cut out mainstream media and television. Most Americans spend an average of four to five hours a day watching television. That's over two months of television per year. Be mindful of what you consume, so you can eliminate the trash coming into your mind. "Garbage in, garbage out." If you decide to watch something, try a documentary or a show that elevates your heart and mind. A great film that does both is *My Octopus Teacher* on Netflix. Gaia TV also offers many films to choose from.

Here are some inspiring films that have helped me: *Winged Migration, Planet Earth II, Kiss the Ground, Inner Worlds and Outer Worlds,* and *The Miracle Morning Movie.*

CONSIDER A 12-STEP PROGRAM

> *This program is simple and it works well with complex people. It is made up of ancient but timeless principles: overcome the ego, connect to a Higher Self, [connect to] a higher purpose, and serve others.*[14]

> Russell Brand

Elevating your recovery might include working a 12-Step program. I've been a member of a 12-Step program for over a decade. Twelve-step groups were a mandatory part of my court sentencing in early recovery. I discovered strong support for recovery in these communities. My weekly commitment to attend meetings and find connection was instrumental to my recovery process.

As I mentioned earlier, I entered a serious relationship about two years into recovery. The problem was that I had not done the work on myself to be healthy in a relationship. The result was jealousy, bitterness, envy, sex addiction, and manipulation. I became physically ill and experienced a hard emotional bottom. After the breakup, I showed up to a 12-Step meeting and asked for help through the 12 Steps.

A few years later, the pain of my past returned, and I began taking the 12 Steps more seriously. The 12-Step program helped me look the world in the eye again, especially through the amends process in steps 8 and 9. I made amends for the damage I caused to employers, family, and friends during active addiction.

For example, twelve years into my recovery, I went to Walmart to make amends. I spoke to a manager named Antonio about how I had used counterfeit money during my active addiction to buy a product and return it for real money. I was fearful, but then something unexpected happened. Antonio explained to me that his mother had been struggling with addiction, and he was not sure what to do. I went from being full of fear to being full of compassion. He told me to call back on Monday morning so he could speak with upper management about the situation. Upper management decided that the best way to complete the amends was to donate the money to a local charity Walmart supported. Experiences like this made the 12 Steps a healing, humbling, and rewarding experience. My amends process continues to this day.

Don't get me wrong, the 12 Steps are a lot of work. I was fortunate to have a loving sponsor named Andrew who'd been down a similar path and was willing to help. The 12-Step program may not be for everyone, but I would strongly consider this option in early recovery. The key to success is your willingness to listen, to be open-minded, and to work the program. A 12-Step program can be used for all addictions, including alcohol, cocaine, heroin, sex, food, gaming, codependent relationships, smoking, gambling, and more. I met most of my recovery team in 12-Step support groups.

> **Action Step:**
>
> Consider joining a 12-Step program. Go to intherooms.com to find a live online meeting or a face-face meeting. In The Rooms® have meetings for people in recovery, people seeking help with an addiction, and for the ally, friend or family member.

ELEVATE YOUR CIRCLE

*Surround yourself with people who remind you
more of your future than of your past.*

Dan Sullivan

One of my first mentors was Pastor Bob. Pastor Bob was a powerful example of a heart-centered male leader. He was a father figure and the role model I lacked growing up. When faced with an impending prison sentence, Pastor Bob provided support and guidance about the potential outcomes of going to prison and not going to prison. He reminded me that no matter what happened, I would get through it. He told me I had a strength called *discernment*, and that this strength would never let me down. I used discernment to advocate for my recovery and freedom. Today I would call it intuition.

Mentors like Pastor Bob love helping because they enjoy seeing people who are willing to change become successful. You can find mentors of your own at work, school, support groups, mastermind groups, events, and volunteer organizations. Mentors are individuals further along the path who can help you navigate obstacles and see new perspectives. Surrounding myself with mentors provided the confidence I needed to start my own business three years ago. Since I had made it through the throws of addiction, I trusted that resilience and support would get me through the challenges of starting a business. I told myself that if I failed, I could always go back to working a job.

Then I joined a personal development mastermind group with my friend Pete. At the first event in Austin, we connected with many successful entrepreneurs who shared about their businesses. Their stories inspired Pete and me to think about becoming entrepreneurs in recovery. As we waited inside the Austin airport for our flight back home, one of the members of the mastermind handed me a small notecard and asked me to write down my biggest goal of the year. The first thing I wrote was "write a book," but then I crossed it out. Then I wrote down "write two books" but crossed it out. I needed a goal that scared the heck out of me, one that seemed impossible. I finally wrote, "Leave my 9–5 job/Be my own boss by August 30, 2017." It was an outrageous goal because I had only five months to make it happen. I had zero experience owning a business. In addition, I had just landed my "dream job" at work, which took twelve years to achieve.

...live a self-directed life,
and strive to reach their full potential.

SAMHSA

If you asked me if I was happy at my current job, I would have told you yes. I didn't want to appear ungrateful. But deep down I was unhappy. I allowed myself to set an unreasonable goal because if I had made it through all of life's adversities up to this point, why couldn't I at least try? If I dedicated myself to my recovery toolkit and continued to learn from mentors, I could make it happen. I placed my small goal card in a spot where I could see it and read it every day.

On August 25, 2017, I worked my last day as a nine-to-five employee. I named my new business Entrepreneurs in Recovery. Entrepreneurs in Recovery would empower people to move out of a cycle of destructive hopelessness and help them harness their unique stories and strengths to build healthy, purpose-driven habits. My mission was to elevate the lives of people in addiction and mental health recovery who are lost, stuck, and lack direction to gain clarity and live a life of purpose. Yet again, what was once impossible was now a reality. Every day, I wake up with energy, passion, and excitement to serve others. Of course, there are challenges, but anything is possible when you focus on your recovery and surround yourself with people who inspire you.

Now it's your turn. Start to think about people who excel at what you want to do in the future. You can find mentors to help you with your finances, health, fitness, relationships, spirituality, business, and career. For example, if you want to learn how to start a recovery coaching business, choose a mentor who's already accomplished this and reach out to them. You might already have mentors in your life you can ask. Mentors do not have to be alive. I have mentors who passed away years ago, such as Wayne Dyer, Carl Jung, and Louise L. Hay. I consider them my mentors because I can access their words through books, lectures, and audios.

Action Step:

Take a moment to list 3 to 5 mentors, role models, teachers, or inspiring people to learn from:

1.

2.

3.

4.

5.

We can stand on the shoulders of our mentors. Mentors inspire us to become the greatest version of ourselves. They're a powerful resource of wisdom and development for your recovery journey. Start by contacting one mentor at a time. In time you might have over fifty mentors. Be sure to learn all you can about your mentor before reaching out to them. Read their books, watch their videos, attend their events, and become a student of their work. Continually find a way to add value to your mentors.

ELEVATE YOUR VISION

Begin with the end in mind.

Stephen R. Covey

Visualization is a practice that elevates our recovery because our imagination is a powerful tool for inspiration, creation, and design. When I practice visualization, it helps me relax and focus on what matters most. Some of the most respected and successful leaders, athletes, and entrepreneurs practice visualization to improve their performance. Visualization helps you see and/or feel a goal being completed by creating positive images of a new future. The key to practicing visualization is to let go of all attachment to a specific outcome. After I visualize, I let go and trust I will be supported with my goals and intentions.

My first use of visualization was at my job at Verizon Wireless. I set a goal to win the highest award in the company called President's Cabinet. This award is given to 0.7 percent of the entire company. After a year of working hard, practicing visualization, and following a plan of action, I did not win the award. But at the end of the following year, I received the news that I was ranked as most likely to win this prestigious award. Once again, I began visualizing every detail of the event. Here was my visualization: *I'm sitting in a beautiful room waiting for my name to be called at the Badrutt's Palace in St. Moritz, Switzerland. My emotions are pure joy, excitement, and gratitude. I hear my name being announced. I begin walking towards the stage with a smile on my face—savoring every moment of the experience. I walk up to the president and accept my award. I pause for a moment to honor this achievement and to show appreciation.*

In March 2016, my vision was accomplished. I flew to St. Moritz, Switzerland, with my best friend Pete. The award ceremony in Badrutt's Palace was stunning. After a short period of time, my name was announced, and Pete started recording the moment on his cell phone. I made my way to the stage with a big smile on my face. Just writing this brings a huge wave of emotions. I shook the vice president's hand first, then the president's hand. I still watch Pete's recording as a reminder of how powerful recovery is.

NOT ONLY IS RECOVERY POSSIBLE, IT WILL BRING YOU TO PLACES YOU CAN ONLY IMAGINE.

This event marked a huge turning point in my professional career.

Here's one more example of practicing visualization. While attending my first mastermind event, I met an entrepreneur named Julie Reisler. During our first conversation, Julie shared that she had a vision of me speaking on stage at an event called The Best Year Ever Blueprint. What's interesting is Pete and I attended this event a year prior. Pete shared with me a similar vision he'd had a few months earlier. These two experiences provided the inspiration I needed. I started my daily visualization practice. Here's what I visualized: *I stand patiently awaiting my name to be called to the stage. The host Hal Elrod introduces me and invites me to come up to the stage. I confidently make my way up towards the stage with a smile. The crowd is sending me tons of support and positive energy. I deliver my story of recovery with power, ease, and grace. I receive a standing ovation.*

I know it sounds simple. Sometimes I added more detail, but the theme remained the same. I repeated this visualization every morning for six months straight. At this point, the event was only a few weeks away, and I had not heard a thing about being a guest to speak. Then, five days before the event, I got an email asking if I would be a speaker. During my talk, I shared how I had visualized this exact moment. I shared my addiction recovery story with over four hundred people and received a standing ovation. Several people approached me afterwards to share about a family member or friend who was battling addiction. They said my story gave them hope.

Go confidently in the direction of your dreams.
Live the life you have imagined.

Henry David Thoreau

I love practicing visualization when I work with people in addiction and mental health recovery. I help guide participants in imagining themselves co-creating their future and creating a small action plan.

Below is a visualization for you to try. I recommend playing calming music with no lyrics to support you in the process. Make sure you have a notebook and pen in order to journal after you finish the visualization. This visualization will take about four to five minutes. Take your time reading each question out loud.

HERE'S A VISUALIZATION TO USE FOR YOUR FUTURE VISION:

Start playing your calming music.

Begin by taking three or four deep breaths into your heart or chest area. Get your feet flat on the floor, relax, and get comfortable. Close your eyes, if you feel comfortable doing so.

Imagine your life one year from today. Your life has truly transformed. Everything you thought was possible for your life and recovery is now happening.

What images are you seeing?

What experiences are you having?

Who are you with?

What conversations are you having?

What types of fun are you having?

What images give you the greatest sense of hope, joy, meaning, purpose, and fulfillment? What images make you fully come alive?

When you finish your visualization, immediately grab a pen and write down everything you saw. If you saw an image, picture, or symbol, draw it. Don't edit anything. Just write down everything that came to you. After about five to ten minutes of writing, pause and take a look at what you've written or created. If you are guiding this visualization in a group, ask the group to find a partner. Each partner will take turns sharing what they wrote down. After a person shares for five minutes, have their partner reflect back appreciation, and then switch.

You might be saying to yourself, "I can't visualize. I don't see anything when I close my eyes." I get it. In the beginning I had a very hard time seeing images. For me, I tend to sense and feel more than I see images.

It's also important to note that not all of my visualizations materialize. In fact, what I visualize often changes into something greater than I could have imagined. What's important is to practice visualization, let go of the outcome, and take note of what you're learning about yourself, others, and the world.

Action Step:

Our imagination is a tool. Practice the visualization I provided above and write down everything you experienced during your visualization in a journal.

Then, ask yourself:

What do I want to be celebrating one year from now?

What's the simplest action I can take today to make my vision a reality?

Important tip: Be careful whom you share your vision with. Most people are not working towards their purpose or dream, so they might bring you down when you share yours. Choose the person you confide in carefully.

ELEVATE YOUR GOALS AND INTENTIONS

We don't have an attention deficit disorder; we have an intention deficit disorder.

Michael Beckwith

Many goals I choose seem unreasonable at the time. An example is this book you're now reading. I placed a picture of this book on my vision board for three years before it came to pass. Be patient with yourself. Write your goals and intentions down and place them on a vision board where you can see them. Start with small daily actions, stay persistent, and ask for help. If a goal does not come to pass, don't be discouraged. You've become a more resilient person as a result of pursuing your goals. Now that you have your vision, it's time to create a plan of action.

Action Step:

Use what you wrote down from your visualization to help you design your vision board. Give yourself permission to think even bigger than you ever have before. Don't be ashamed to place things on your vision board like a new Tesla, a five-bedroom house on the ocean, or becoming a world-renowned musician or speaker. If these are things you want, then they belong on your vision board. Look through magazines or search the internet for images of places you want to visit, live events you want to attend, or items you want to have. Cut out or print the images and place them on your vision board. Or, if you're artistic, go ahead and draw your images.

Next, write down empowering words of inspiration or quotes from your favorite speakers, authors, or mentors. Add these words to your vision board. Add your own words of wisdom as well. Once your vision board is full of images and quotes, place it in a location you can see every day. I like to place my vision board next to my dedicated meditation spot. Update your vision board every three to six months.

Every day, ask yourself this question: What one thing can I do, no matter how small, that would help elevate my recovery?

CHAPTER 7

APPRECIATE YOUR RECOVERY

I've learned that people will forget what you said, people will forget what you did, but people will never forget how you made them feel.

Maya Angelou

The third part of the FEARS recovery toolkit is to *appreciate your recovery*. When we show appreciation for our recovery, we improve our physical, emotional, spiritual, and mental well-being. Appreciating your recovery involves making a gratitude list, journaling, affirmations, appreciating your story, forgiveness, sharing your story, and being of service to others. The more you appreciate your recovery, the more abundance you'll experience. Abundance is the sun shining on your face, breathing in the fresh air, food in your refrigerator, and people who support your recovery. Many people do not have the privilege of experiencing these simple luxuries. Because recovery gives us a do-over, we can start to appreciate things we once took for granted. Let's take a deep dive into the actions for appreciating your recovery.

START YOUR DAY WITH GRATITUDE

> *Gratitude is the law of increase, and complaint is the law of decrease.*
>
> Florence Scovel Shinn

Journaling is a necessary part of my recovery. When Pastor Bob asked me to start journaling during my first week of recovery, I purchased a blue notebook and wrote down the things I was grateful for and my experiences from the day. When things didn't go my way, I would write it down in my journal and be thankful for another day of recovery. If I didn't have my journal with me, I would write on anything I could find. No matter what, I took the time to write down my gratitude and thoughts for the day.

Here's an excerpt from my first journal:

Journal Entry from January 8, 2006

20 Days in Recovery:

Justin and I spent the evening at my company's New Year's Eve party. What a wonderful night we had together while my brother got to meet my friends I have worked with for nearly two years. Thank you so much for this night, God. I know such nice people. Life is very delicate and precious. This night has reminded me of this. Faithfulness and Believing.

At the beginning of recovery, what helped me most were simple daily practices like journaling. Besides focusing on my recovery, working hard at my job, and attending 12-Step groups after work or on my days off, I would put my pen to paper every day. Journaling is therapeutic. I wrote down my experiences with panic attacks, depression, and a pending prison sentence, as well as my gratitude. My mental, emotional, and spiritual well-being are connected to my daily journaling routine. More recently, I began keeping a small journal in my bathroom to write down three things I'm grateful for before taking a cold shower. Author James Clear calls this practice *habit stacking*, where you find a habit you already do (cold shower) and stack a habit on top of it (gratitude journaling).[15] This practice is particularly useful for people in early recovery, since we greatly benefit from keeping things simple.

Action Step:

Start a gratitude journaling routine. Write down 3–5 things you appreciate about yourself, the day ahead of you, or anything you feel grateful for. Do this every morning for the next 30 days after you wake up or before you jump in the shower. If you need more inspiration, go outside into nature to write your gratitude list.

APPRECIATE YOUR SELF-TALK

The deepest principle of human nature is a craving to be appreciated.

William James

The words we use to talk to ourselves matter. Growing up, I constantly worried something bad was going to happen. Even when things were going well, my mind would find something to worry about. When I was in active addiction, I would numb my worries and anxiety. As soon as I sobered up, the remorse, shame, and dread would return again. My self-talk at the time sounded like, "What's the point of even trying to quit? If someone had my life, they would be getting messed up too. It is what it is, I've just accepted it. My father was an addict, so I'm an addict." Negative self-talk led to actions that were destroying my life.

My self-talk didn't change when I found recovery. I would think to myself, "You will always be defined as an addict or a felon. People will look down at you if you tell them you're in recovery. You could have done more. You could have done it better. You will never be okay."

Our mind's default is to focus on the negative or search for a problem instead of a solution to keep the drama going. Negativity is normal if you read the news or surround yourself with negative people. Since feeling angry or depressed about my past no longer served my highest good, I needed to change the way I talked to myself.

During my pretrial, Pastor Bob gifted me a miniature Bible. He would highlight verses to read before meeting my lawyer, on important court dates, or before bed. I memorized these verses and repeated them to myself all day long. The method I used to remember verses and affirmations was to write them down at the bottom of my journal every day. One of my first affirmations was, "For I know the plans I have for you, declares the Lord, plans to prosper you and not to harm you, plans to give you hope and a future" (Jeremiah 29:11). Facing legal pressure and panic attacks made me willing to try new things. My panic attacks would happen at work without my permission; I felt like I was going to die. I would try calming myself by saying to myself, "I'm here. I'm okay. I'm going to be okay."

Affirmations are a kind of self-talk that is true for you in the moment. Remember writing your purpose statement in chapter 5? Your purpose statement is an affirmation you can repeat daily. You can also use "I am" statements like "I am resilient," "I am whole," "I am love," and "I am bold."

My friend and mentor Hal Elrod, author of the life changing and bestselling book *The Miracle Morning*, is a great source for affirmations. For example, Hal says, "How you start your day determines how you create your life, because your day is your life." Your affirmations can be as long or short as you choose, as long as they resonate with you.

If you're currently struggling with anxiety, low self-esteem, self-doubt, and low self-worth, start repeating supportive affirmations daily. Write in your journal what you appreciate about yourself, such as "I appreciate my smile," "I love my drive and motivation to help others," "I appreciate my recovery," and "I love my sense of humor."

In his book *Love Yourself Like Your Life Depends on It*, author Kamal Ravikant shares his "I love myself" meditation. The instructions are to repeat "I love myself" for five minutes while looking at yourself in the bathroom mirror.[16] When we love ourselves, we radiate this love to others. We don't have to look outside ourselves for approval because everything we need is inside. After a few months of this practice, I started to become more relaxed around people.

Action Step:

Write down your affirmations. Use "I am" statements, such as "I am bold," "I am resilient," or "I am compassion." Some other examples are "I choose recovery," "I choose to be healthy," or "I choose to be grateful today."

Repeat your affirmations in the morning after your meditation, during a shower, on your drive to work, and before going to bed.

Say your affirmation(s) out loud every day for the next 30 days.

APPRECIATE YOUR STORY

When you forgive, you don't change the past.
You change the future.

Judith Orloff, MD

Many of us live with shame from our past, which keeps us stuck. We avoid confronting our shame by covering it with food, drugs, sex, alcohol, people pleasing, technology, and any other addiction. If you feel this way, you are not alone! We are only as sick as our secrets. I was ashamed my family had to see me handcuffed in court. I was ashamed I flunked out of college and failed to help my single mom while I was in active addiction. I was also ashamed of my mental health conditions. It was not until I became vulnerable and willing to share my shame with safe people that I learned about self-forgiveness.

Being vulnerable takes tremendous courage. I attribute my greatest healing and growth to moments of vulnerability, when I asked for help or when I shared my story with someone. My story contains all of me, including my addictions, messiness, failures, successes, inadequacies, embarrassing moments, and screwups.

You might not love yourself at the moment, but I love you. I will love you until you can love yourself. Why? Because that's what happened to me. You can start to love and forgive yourself by sharing your story with someone you can trust. The first person I shared my story with was my therapist Bonnie. For you, it might be a sponsor, a close friend in recovery, a mentor, or a spiritual advisor. Sharing your story will help you start experiencing good feelings again.

You have been criticizing yourself for years, and it hasn't
worked. Try approving of yourself and see what happens.

Louise L. Hay

I was just over a year in recovery when the news came that I was not going to federal prison. During my final court appearance, my lawyer asked if I wanted to share anything with the judge. My answer was a resounding yes because I wanted to advocate for recovery. As I stood before the judge with my family standing close by, fear was ever present, but I shared my story and expressed appreciation for all the challenges and successes that first year of recovery. My willingness to ask for help, take small daily actions, and listen to people who knew about a path of recovery paid off.

Everything happens in life for a reason—even my father leaving when I was four years old and facing federal felonies at the age of twenty-two. If it weren't for those circumstances, this book you are now reading would not exist. I might have never found recovery or practiced self-care like my life depended on it. My adversities shaped my resilience and character. We can choose to live a life of fear, anger, and shame, or we can choose to live with love, forgiveness, and self-compassion. Make a conscious choice to learn from the past and share your experience whenever you can be of service.

You are the co-creator of your life story. If you don't believe your story matters, that's okay. If you're a person who has overcome addiction, trauma, adversity, and/or mental health conditions, then you have a powerful story of transformation. Your story will become a great gift to the people you choose to share it with. How you overcame adversities despite life's challenges will become a guidepost for those still sick and suffering. The tools within this book will help you create a new story. You have the power to change the rest of your story.

Action Step:

Write down the people you need to forgive in your journal. Make sure you include yourself in the list. Write down how you were hurt by this person. Now, write what your part was in each situation. Write a statement of forgiveness for each person on your list. The last step is for you to write down your gratitude and appreciation for the lesson or the insight you gained from this situation or experience. Finally, tear the page up into pieces and discard it in the trash. Repeat this process as often as you need to.

APPRECIATE YOUR STORY

My journal is my secret weapon.

Yanik Silver

Journaling is a creative way to appreciate your story. Because I don't always get to share my emotions with people during the day, I write down my thoughts, feelings, and emotions at the end of the day. Since I tend to be closed off about my personal life, I choose to write down my thoughts and share them with people on my recovery team. This helps me grow closer to the people I care about. For example, I have a lifelong habit of unconsciously grabbing my left arm whenever I'm overthinking or nervous. I hid this obsessive-compulsive behavior for over twenty-five years. I decided to share this fact about myself with a friend on my recovery team. This opened the door for me to share aspects of myself that my ego judges as weird, strange, shameful, and unlovable.

Action Step:

Write down your story in your journal. First, write down your accomplishments, no matter how small they seem. Then capture all of your adversities, challenges, traumas, and moments of resilience. Don't edit anything. Get it all on paper. It might take you a few days. When you feel like you've got it all written down, schedule a time to share your story with a therapist, a close recovery friend, or a spiritual advisor.

SHARE YOUR STORY

Connection is the energy that is created between people when they feel seen, heard, and valued, when they can give and receive without judgment.

Brené Brown

My work as a recovery facilitator allows me to hear incredible stories from people in addiction and mental health recovery.

SHARING STORIES HELPS PEOPLE FLOURISH IN RECOVERY.

By sharing their stories, the men and women I work with discover they already have everything they need to learn, heal, and grow. When I met Vincent during his stay at an inpatient treatment center for drugs and alcohol, he was a few weeks sober. Vincent suffered from mental health challenges, as well as substance use disorder. During his time in treatment, he experienced two of my recovery workshops. I bumped into Vincent three months after treatment when I was running another workshop at his sober living residence. He was still in recovery and doing great. Vincent shared with me how my workshops helped motivate him to seek work in the addiction recovery field. He recently celebrated two years of recovery and is now working for the same treatment center he attended.

Vincent stated, "I loved the structure of the recovery workshops. I was able to connect to other people in my group. I never would have chosen to work with this person I was paired with, but I learned that each of us possesses our own skills. Recovery can be like a Swiss Army knife, a tool that can fix many things. I've seen the workshop encourage people to share things they wouldn't have shared in other groups at the treatment center." Vincent is currently working towards becoming an expressive therapist.

You can't make anyone choose recovery; you can only share your experiences. When we share our story or listen compassionately to someone else's story, we recognize we are more similar than we are different. We all experience loneliness, pain, tragedy, and change. We are all connected at an energetic level. Our moments of darkness have not been wasted. People will thank you for sharing your authentic self with them. We have a responsibility to those we can serve, so do not let your story go untold. Seeing a person who was once ravaged by addiction and mental health challenges begin to prosper is one of the greatest treasures of recovery. The more you share your story, the more momentum you'll create. Finding your voice will inspire others to find theirs.

> **Action Step:**
>
> Sharing your story connects you to a higher purpose. Ask yourself, "How can I use my story and experiences to serve others?" Volunteer to share your story at a local sober living residence, a treatment center, or a support group.

Every day, ask yourself this question: "What one thing can I do, no matter how small, to appreciate my recovery?"

CHAPTER 8

RESILIENCE IN RECOVERY

Everything can be taken from a man but one thing:
the last of the human freedoms—
to choose one's attitude in any given set of circumstances,
to choose one's own way.

Victor Frankl

The fourth part of the FEARS recovery toolkit is *resilience in recovery*. Recovery requires resilience. Resilience in recovery is about overcoming adversity, developing a resilient heart and mind, facing our fears, and trusting our intuition. We use resilience to survive the low spots, setbacks, and adversities we encounter during our recovery journey. Can you think of a time when you've been resilient? When we take a closer look, we begin noticing certain inner strengths emerging during challenges, hardships, and adversities. The most common strength I've found to be universal with people in recovery is resilience.

Resilience in recovery is needed because addiction is life or death. When I worked as a clinical mental health counselor for the Hillsboro County Drug Court, three clients overdosed and passed away within a six-month period. For those working on the front lines of the addiction crisis, life has become arduous and heartbreaking. Today a single shot of heroin can be fatal. As I write these words, I'm preparing for a funeral for a friend who recently overdosed. During the COVID-19 pandemic, the world of mental health and addiction has worsened, and some say this is the worst mental health crisis of our time. It's become a pandemic of isolation.

This pandemic is a true test of our resilience in recovery. Many people have reached out for help during this time, even friends with decades of recovery. I've also reached out to my recovery team for help and reassurance. Remember to lean on your recovery team for support.

LEVERAGE YOUR INNER POWER

Resilience: the capacity to prepare for, recover from, and adapt in the face of stress, challenge or adversity.

HeartMath Institute

As you've learned from reading this book, being in recovery is much more than avoiding behaviors and substances that bring you harm. Recovery is about being resilient during life's challenges, co-creating a life you desire, and reaching your full potential. Resilience in recovery is a reminder that hardships will come, but we *will* make it through.

The book you are now reading is an idea I had over ten years ago. I've gone back and forth about whether or not to write it. During the writing process, I gave up several times. My thoughts included, "Who are you to write a book about addiction and mental health recovery? People are not going to agree with your version of recovery. People are going to find out who you really are." I felt like an imposter. Discouraged, I would close my laptop in disgust. Months passed by without writing because I let fear and negativity get the best of me. If it were not for the people suffering from addiction and mental health conditions who want nothing more than to find recovery, I would have given up. I received messages from strangers and from parents who feel hopeless because their child or loved one is addicted. I learned about friends from high school who have taken their own life. I was sent text messages about friends passing away from an overdose.

These tragedies kept my heart and mind on track. I refuse to deny anyone an opportunity to hear a message of hope, resilience, and recovery. I've witnessed so many people go from fearful, addicted, and hopeless to healthy, hopeful, and whole. In fact, a few years ago, I met my former drug dealer at a meeting, and he shared with me that he had opened a sober living residence for men. Today he's a successful entrepreneur in recovery, providing addiction treatment for men and women around the country.

Action Step:

Ask yourself the following questions and write your responses in your journal. "What is my most important goal, opportunity, or challenge in the next 90 days that will require resilience?" "What personal practices, habits, or actions can I commit to in order to embody resilience?" "Who will keep me accountable?" You can also add your goal, opportunity, or challenge to your vision board.

DEVELOP A RESILIENT HEART AND MIND

No matter how many times we fall, we get back up.

Resilience in Recovery Workshop participants

How do we unlock our innate resilience? We begin by no longer living with a victim mentality. Life is happening *for* us, not *to* us. You have it in you to change your health and wellness, deal with the repercussions from your past, and move forward towards a full life in recovery. Many people today live with a fear-based mindset, ruled by the opinions of others, and afraid to move out of their comfort zone. When you begin to trust your resilient heart and mind, you focus on yourself instead of trying to fix the world.

Five years into recovery, I decided to Google my name. The top search result displayed an article about my arrest at twenty-two years old. The article was short, but it detailed my sentencing for ordering pharmaceutical medications illegally. I was ashamed and embarrassed. I wanted to tell my story when I was ready, but now anyone could access my past from a Google search. Instead of allowing this article to be a setback, I used it as motivation to exercise my resilient heart and mind to create success in recovery. Today when people search my name, they'll find the work I'm doing as an entrepreneur in recovery.

More than education, more than experience,
more than training, a person's level of resilience
will determine who succeeds and who fails.
That's true in the cancer ward, it's true in the Olympics,
and it's true in the boardroom.[17]

Diane Coutu

When I was growing up, I had an entrepreneurial spirit. It was necessary for me to work at a young age if I wanted nice things. At eleven years old, I held yard sales outside my first-floor apartment. I started delivering newspapers to save up for my first BMX bike, snowboard, and dirt bike. As a teenager, I worked in the electronics department at Staples. This is where I learned I had a knack for selling. In my next job working in cellular phones, I became a top sales rep despite my addiction to opioids. When I got back from Florida, I went to my old employer for a job. A few weeks later I was arrested. When my boss got the call that I had been in trouble, he still hired me because of the success I'd had in the past. Instead of doing what was expected of me, I went above and beyond by creating a list of twenty actions I needed to accomplish every day to do my personal best. After attending college in recovery for ten years, I completed my undergraduate and graduate degrees. I don't share this to brag, but to show you what's possible with a resilient heart and mind.

If you want to develop a resilient heart and mind and make your future greater than your past, focus on what you're passionate about and surround yourself with people that inspire you. I'm passionate about facilitating life-changing conversations in the world of addiction and mental health recovery. What I do doesn't feel like work because I experience a sense of flow and a sense of purpose.

Action Step:

Ask yourself the following questions and write your responses in your journal. "When in my life have I overcome some type of obstacle, challenge, adversity, hardship or difficulty? How did I overcome it? How did I bounce back from it?" As you reflect on this story, write down 1–2 of your greatest qualities or inner strengths that were present when you overcame this adversity or challenge. Maybe you're courageous, intuitive, persistent, bold, resilient, a risk-taker, compassionate, empathetic, driven, or determined. Now create a resilience affirmation using 10–12 of the words you wrote.

For example, "No matter how many times I fall, I get back up." "My courage and determination help me follow my heart to reach my goals." "When I look deep within, I was born for this shit." "No matter what life throws me, I won't give up." "I'm a force for good, and I will not quit."

Write your resilience affirmation here:

Important tip: Place your resilience affirmation on the back of your cell phone, in your wallet, or on your bathroom mirror and repeat it every day for the next thirty days.

FACE YOUR FEAR

Fear is something you will face
right before you give up or overcome.

Andre Norman

What does fear mean? Some say false evidence appearing real, fantasized experiences appearing real, f*ck everything and run, for everything a reason, or face everything and recover. Have you ever faced a fear and succeeded? When you walk through a fear, you are being resilient. But fear often causes us to feel stuck, afraid, lost, or hopeless. Those of us who struggle with addiction and mental health conditions often fear the unknown. We fear what will happen if we stop using our drug of choice. We fear life will be boring without our addiction to rely upon. We fear that if we quit, our pain will return. These are normal fears. I recently received my father's death certificate. The first word stated as the cause of his death was "alcoholic." I'm choosing to break the bondage of addiction in my family lineage. I choose to focus, elevate, appreciate, build resilience, and practice self-care in recovery. I choose to let go of rigidity. I choose to face my fears and get out of my comfort zone.

FACING FEAR IS NOT EASY, BUT YOU CAN DO *ANYTHING* BECAUSE YOU ARE RESILIENT.

The key is to take it one step at a time. Whether you've been to jail, faced a near-death experience, or overcome a major adversity, your resilience opens up a portal of hope. When we find recovery, we sometimes get disturbed by minor inconveniences compared to the difficulties we faced during our addiction. For example, I got a C on a paper my first year in recovery. I was angry and then depressed at the thought of failing out of college again. Then I remembered how I almost lost my life to addiction a few months before taking this class. My grades in school were not as important as my recovery. Remembering where we've come from keeps us on the path of progress, not perfection.

You will face many challenges in life and recovery. I was told having felonies would cause me to struggle to find employment. This was not exactly encouraging news. I could have made these people right and sold myself short. I'm actually grateful for these people because they gave me the motivation to go back to school to complete my degree. What I learned later on is I didn't need a degree to be successful and feel okay. In fact, some of the most successful people on earth never earned a college degree. I'm not saying education is not important, because a degree can pay off. I just want you to be aware that you have options. You can start a business or find meaningful work without having a degree.

My friend Pete is a great example of someone who chose to find meaningful work instead of a college degree. Pete was a daily IV heroin user for over seven years. I met Pete in recovery when he was working for a company making twelve dollars an hour. He eventually worked his way up to become an HVAC tech making thirty-five dollars an hour for many years of his recovery. Today Pete has a beautiful family and runs his own successful HVAC company as an entrepreneur in recovery. Whether you're ready to face your fears and find a pathway to recovery or not, I'm grateful to be here with you. Remember, failure is a stepping-stone to greatness. You're exactly where you are supposed to be at this moment.

The greatest gift you can give somebody
is your own personal development.
I used to say, "If you will take care of me,
I will take care of you."
Now I say, "I will take care of me for you,
if you will take care of you for me."

Jim Rohn

In 2016, I created a Facebook group to record short motivational videos with a group of friends. My goal was to overcome my fear of embarrassment of being seen on video. The feedback from my first few videos was positive. A week into my challenge, I shot a video on my way to work and uploaded it to Facebook. As I walked into work, I checked Facebook and noticed 33 notifications. That was strange. It turned out my video was accidentally shared to my main news feed instead of my secret Facebook group. I instantly felt a huge wave of shame and embarrassment. As I went to delete the video as quickly as possible, I noticed dozens of comments, such as "This is amazing!" "I needed this today." "Where are the other videos?!" My fear of embarrassment in sharing my voice with the world disappeared at that moment. I started posting videos for anyone to watch. The quality of the videos wasn't great, but that's not the point. The point is I would rather look weird at times and live my dreams than live a life of regret and wonder *what if?*

Action Step:

It takes courage to do the next right thing every day. It also takes courage to face your fears and embrace discomfort. Choose one action today that's out of your comfort zone. Ask for help, ask someone to be on your recovery team, take a different route to work, forgive someone, write a blog and share it with the world, take a cold shower—anything that feels uncomfortable but will allow you to grow.

Important tip: Repeat the affirmation, "I choose to do the next right thing."

TRUST YOUR INTUITION

*Our heart is our intuitive feeling center
and source of intuition.*

Dr. Rollin McCraty

Have you ever had a strong inner knowing and ignored it? When I was sending money to Western Union to order prescription pills, I chose to ignore my inner voice and paid a heavy price for it. When I chose to leave my nine-to-five job, people thought I was crazy. Why would you leave a secure job of fourteen years with no guarantee of success? Once again, I leaned into my resilience and trusted my intuition. I had to trust and respect my inner knowing more than the opinions of others, even when I didn't know what would happen.

Two months after I left my job, I enrolled in a training course that led to the exact work I'm doing today with recovery facilitation. How was I supposed to know this training would appear when I made my decision to leave my job? When you walk out in faith and trust your intuition, you reap the rewards. Intuition is one of the greatest gifts of my recovery.

Trusting your intuition adds to your resilience. I choose to let my intuition guide my most important decisions in recovery. Trusting our inner knowing doesn't mean we ignore our mind. Our mind is important, but most of us spend way too much time in our heads. We live our lives according to the logic of the brain, ignoring our deep inner knowing.

Intuition is not limited to a religion or belief system. Every person has access to their intuition. Some people call it trusting their heart. We can use our intuitive insights to make decisions in a more discerning way. Intuition can even enhance one's recovery. In a study of twelve individuals in recovery from alcoholism, participants claimed that intuition "initiated, sustained, and enhanced their sobriety."[18]

Since women tend to have strong intuition, it's my goal to help more men trust their inner voice. When I learned to trust my intuition, I began to let go and trust that I was doing the next right thing. In my first full year as an entrepreneur in recovery, I made $9,000. The struggle was real, but my mission was to help five thousand men and women in addiction and mental health recovery learn purpose-driven habits in order to thrive. I eventually managed to pay all my bills for three months in a row and continue this momentum. This was the confirmation I needed that following my intuition was the right decision. Are you willing to trust your intuition to help enhance your recovery and find work you're passionate about?

The gift of synchronicity is a birthright given to all of us.
Whether you collect that gift is entirely up to you.

Dr. Philip Merry

Here are some examples of what I write in my journal:

Monday, February 18, 2019: *Full moon*

At 11:11 p.m., I was writing in my book about my father's death certificate, when I experienced a strong feeling my dad was the one who helped me get arrested at the post office to save me from further destruction. Since he wasn't able to help me when he was alive, he helped me on the other side.

Saturday, April 27, 2019

My flight number to LA was 2220. I sent a text to Julie when I landed at 2:22 p.m.

Later that evening, I spoke with Charlie at Canter's. When he told me he was 9 months sober, his watch read 22:22.

Start to become aware of experiences, signs, and synchronicities, such as seeing the number 11:11 or 2:22 appear on a clock, or seeing license plates with the numbers 333, 444, or 555 a few times on a drive. I often see certain birds like blue jays, cardinals, hawks, or the occasional bald eagle when I'm thinking of people or ideas. A month before COVID-19 started, I drove two hours to purchase a car. During my drive, I began doubting whether buying a new car was the right decision. In that exact moment, I saw a bald eagle resting on a tree branch. To me, this was confirmation I was on the right path.

Action Step:

In your journal, write down the times when you trust your heart, intuition, or inner knowing. Also record any out of the blue experiences, synchronicities, or meaningful coincidences. You can even record your dreams. Do this every day for the next 2 weeks.

Every day, ask yourself this question: What one thing can I do, no matter how small, that would increase my confidence and resilience in recovery?

CHAPTER 9

SELF-CARE IN RECOVERY

Self-care is not selfish.

Source Unknown

Self-care in recovery is the fifth part of the FEARS recovery toolkit. But this does not mean self-care comes last. When it comes to self-care, I recommend a holistic approach, just as I do with recovery. I've become a strong advocate for self-care because of the deep level of healing it has provided. In our high-paced society, it's easy to ignore our needs and get lost in the rat race of life. We need to slow down! When we slow down, we recharge our inner battery before helping others.

IF WE WANT TO EXPERIENCE OPTIMAL HEALTH AND WELLNESS IN RECOVERY, WE MUST MAKE SELF-CARE A PRIORITY.

If you were like me, you probably disregarded self-care during active addiction. Now I start every day with self-care. If I miss my self-care practices, my reaction to people, places, and things begin to deteriorate. Depression and anxiety return. The people around me begin asking, "Is everything ok?" which leads to resentment. When my pain, irritability, and discomfort peaks, this is usually when I pause and do a self-check in. I take a rest for five to ten minutes and practice meditation, a mindfulness technique, or ten to twenty deep heart-focused breaths with my eyes closed. This moment of rest is a reset button for my day.

Also, when I began eating foods higher in nutrition and stopped addictive substances like caffeine, dairy products, and white sugar, it made a noticeable improvement to my mental, physical, emotional, and spiritual life. When we respect our mind, body, and spirit, we experience greater self-esteem, appreciation, and healing. Becoming angry or frustrated with yourself is normal in early recovery, but as you practice self-care on a daily basis, your reactions to life begin to change. For example, when someone did not respond to my phone call or text message, it infuriated me because it triggered past hurt. As I learned to self-regulate with self-care and develop an awareness of these past hurts, I was able to change my response. Most of the time, it's none of my business why someone isn't responding to me. They might be busy with a sick child or parent, or just busy with their own life.

My suggestion is to give yourself permission to feel good, but don't expect to be perfect with self-care. You're allowed to have a bad day once in a while. People assume I rarely struggle with my mental health because I've dedicated my life to this work, but this is far from the truth. Once in a while, I lose my shit, have a pity party for one, and cry out to the world how I've been wronged. During 2020, my old thoughts of hopelessness and depression returned, and I felt like I was moving backwards. What kept me sane was staying connected to my recovery team and my dedication to the self-care practices I'm about to teach you.

We all have a self-care bank account that begins to grow during our morning routine. Stress, tension, and energy demands withdraw from our self-care bank account throughout the day. The more you practice self-care and nourish yourself, the more you can withdraw. For example, being around certain people drains my energy. Instead of avoiding them altogether, I practice the Quick Coherence Technique™ before spending time with them. I can use it when I'm with the person as well, since you can do this technique with your eyes open. This technique helps add to my resilience during stressful situations and prevents my energy from being drained. You can skip ahead to the mindfulness and meditation section to learn this technique.

When I decided to become a clinical mental health counselor, I told friends and family I wanted to learn and develop new therapeutic techniques to help improve people's mental health. But truthfully, I wanted to learn and understand how to deal with my own mental health challenges. As a wounded healer, I wanted to answer these questions: "What were the causes of my anxiety, depression, and feelings of unworthiness? Why did life seem so difficult at times? Why did I feel isolated and separate from everyone else?" When I learned a new technique, I experimented on myself first.

One technique for dealing with anxiety was the emotional freedom technique, or tapping, combined with repeating affirmations. I tried this technique every day for a few months. This healing modality helped, but I needed to go a lot further. I began experimenting with mindfulness and meditation, breathing techniques, cold therapy, plant-based foods, movement, and much more. I'm going to help you implement some of these practices into your own self-care regimen.

Self-care in recovery starts by building a daily self-care routine that includes movement, nutrition, rest, honoring our sensitivities, and creating a daily spiritual practice. You can customize your own self-care routine, however you see fit, by adding and subtracting what works for you. I encourage you to experiment with the actions presented in this chapter. I don't expect anyone to implement all of these self-care actions immediately. Start by adding one new practice every other week.

Of course, before you make any changes to your health practices, check with your dietitian or doctor.

GET MOVING

If you have five minutes a day,
you have time to create a healthy habit.[19]

Jaime Hope, MD

Nothing substitutes for good health. If you're not healthy, nothing else matters except returning to health. One of the best ways to be healthy is daily movement and exercise. Exercise is a way to achieve a natural high, reduce depression, and move stress out of your body.[20] When you move your body, you boost your metabolism and release many feel-good chemicals in your brain that can last for hours. These chemicals are known as beta-endorphins. You don't have to become a runner or swim for miles for exercise to be effective. You can keep it simple. Schedule time to go for a ten-minute walk, hike, or a jog every day. Since many of us tend to carry a lot of tension in our bodies ("the issues are in the tissues"), start each day with some simple stretching for five minutes. This is a great way to get your bodily fluids moving and start your morning.

Upon awakening, I stretch for five minutes. Not being able to touch my toes doesn't stop me from trying. I also strength train two to three times a week. Start with a minimum of ten minutes of exercise a day. Find a movement routine that fits your lifestyle. No matter what, get moving!

> **Action Step:**
>
> Choose your favorite exercise: you can take a walk, jog, Samba, hike, trampoline, swim, or dance for 10 minutes a day. By starting with 10 minutes of movement, it guarantees you have the time to exercise. Keep track of your movement routine in your journal.

TAKE COLD SHOWERS

Water contains healing; it is the simplest,
cheapest and—if used correctly—the safest remedy.

Sebastian Kneipp

If you tackle the hardest task first in the morning, you win the day. My hardest task in the morning is a cold shower. You've already learned that cold showers helped me quit caffeine for good. In my first book, *Smash Your Comfort Zone with Cold Showers,* I demonstrated that doing what's uncomfortable builds confidence and helps us reach our full potential. People continually message me about the effectiveness of cold showers and how they help with depression, anxiety, energy, acne, motivation, soreness, immunity, fear, stress, self-confidence, mood, and overall well-being.[21] One of my favorite aspects of cold showers is not getting sick as often, as they have been known to help reduce illness.[22] Using hydrotherapy, including cold showers, as part of my daily self-care routine benefits my recovery and mental health.

A good shock often helps the brain
that has been atrophied by habit.

Napoleon Hill

Action Step:

If you're not sold on the idea of taking a cold shower, start by taking a warm shower, and then turn the water cold for the last 10–15 seconds of your shower. Eventually build your way up to 2 minutes cold. Before you enter the cold water, deepen your breaths—breathe in for 5, hold for 5, breathe out for 7.

Take cold showers every day for the next 7 days. You can try a contrast shower by turning the water hot then cold for a few minutes. Always end your shower cold. If you want a bigger challenge, take a 5-minute cold shower every day for the next 30 days. The most important thing is to use common sense and listen to your body. That said, I've never had anyone tell me taking cold showers for 30 days was a waste of time.

GET SUFFICIENT SLEEP

Despite my years of attempting to be a morning person, I'm still a night person. When most people are sleeping, I find my peace and inspiration. It's nighttime right now as I type these words. Whether you're striving to be part of the 5:00 a.m. club or you're a night owl, make sure you're getting sufficient sleep. When I was working at my job, I told myself I only needed five to six hours of sleep a night. The truth is I need at least seven hours of sleep to feel good and eight hours of sleep to feel excellent. Sufficient sleep has been shown to be beneficial for depression and anxiety as well.[23] Be mindful of how much sleep you need to feel truly rested, renewed, and recharged.

Taking naps or simply resting your eyes is another tool to enhance your self-care routine. When I have a long day, I set my phone's alarm for ten to twenty minutes and rest. When I say rest, I don't necessarily mean I'm sleeping. I'm simply closing my eyes and practicing slow, deep breaths. When I get up, my attitude is improved and my mood is calmer. Rest and recovery are essential to good mental health.

Action Step:

Get sufficient sleep. Learn how much sleep you need to be at your best. If you need 8 hours of sleep, go to bed a little earlier. Also, start taking 10-minute breaks to rest. You don't have to fall asleep. Just allow yourself to slow down and relax.

Important tip: Put your phone in airplane mode before bed and during rest/naps.

NOURISH YOURSELF

Recovery is a process of change through which individuals improve their health and wellness...

SAMHSA

We all most likely neglected to take care of ourselves in active addiction. The foods we chose to eat were less than ideal, and junk food was a big part of the menu. In recovery, we have the opportunity to heal and regenerate ourselves. The foods you put into your mouth affect your energy, thoughts, emotions, motivation, health, and recovery. There's no magic pill that will make you healthy. I was far from a healthy eater growing up and extremely picky. My eating habits carried right into recovery until I started to become aware of how sensitive I was to food. When I started eating plant-based nutrition in 2017, there was a noticeable shift in my energy, mood, and emotions. My daily regimen of fruits, vegetables, smoothies, nuts, seeds, and herbs healed my physical ailments, like debilitating seasonal allergies. Since my health, energy, and recovery are my number one priority, I'm cautious about the foods I consume.

Feeding our bodies with the best possible foods, such as organic fruits and vegetables high in vitamins, minerals, and antioxidants, improves our body's immune system and extends our life.[24] I realize it's not always possible to eat organic, so do your best with what is available to you. You will feel much better overall when you make deliberate food choices.

Foods like meat, dairy, oils, processed foods, refined sugar, and flours are acid-forming foods that cause stagnation and inflammation in your body. Most raw fruits and vegetables are both hydrating and good for your mental health.[25] Eating raw fruits and vegetables, as well as nuts and seeds, has been incredibly beneficial for me during this low-energy period of tension, social distancing, and separation. I started 2020 with a forty-day juice fast to help clear out decades' worth of old waste, toxins, and buildup. I recommend starting with a one-day juice fast and eventually work your way up to three days. However, if you're at risk of an eating disorder, I do not recommend fasting.

In early recovery, drinking Coca-Cola, consuming excessive caffeine, smoking cigarettes, and eating fast food might seem normal for the first few months. But eventually you will want to take a hard look at what you put into your body if you want optimal health in recovery. Changing the way you eat will change the way you feel. Create a wellness plan that includes more plant-based foods in your diet. Use your journal to write down how you feel after each meal.

For example, let's say you just ate a small cheese pizza with some buffalo wings and ranch dipping sauce. Write down how you felt afterwards, especially in terms of your energy level, mood, and motivation. Now try eating a large salad with red peppers, carrots, cucumbers, and homemade avocado dressing. Write down in your journal the way you felt after this meal. Compare your energy levels, mood, and motivation after you consume all meals for the next fourteen days. Tracking your food in this way is how you can know for yourself how your food affects your mood.

Action Step:

Make a smoothie.

My favorite smoothie recipe: 1 cup of frozen or fresh blueberries, 1 ripe mango, 2–3 ripe bananas, 2 dates, 6–8 ounces of unsweetened almond milk or organic coconut water (or don't use any liquids for a thicker smoothie). Blend all of these ingredients together, and you are good to go.

Make a juice.

My favorite simple juice recipe: Add 3–4 apples, a 2-inch piece of ginger, 1 bunch of celery, and 1 whole lemon to your juicer. This makes about 28 ounces of juice. Shoot for all organic ingredients.

Important tip: I recommend purchasing a NutriBullet to get you started. With a NutriBullet, you can make delicious smoothies, dressings, and soups. For a juicer, I recommend starting with a Breville.

STAY HYDRATED

How much water do you drink every day? Most people are walking around dehydrated and don't even know it. I shoot for a minimum of five ounces of water every hour. Water aids in many bodily processes, including moving out toxins. Purchase a thirty-two-ounce bottle, fill it with filtered water, and carry it with you everywhere you go. This will help you stay hydrated throughout the day. Drinking more water will give you more energy. In addition to drinking more water, eating raw fruits is very hydrating since fruits are high in water content. For instance, grapes and apples are over 80 percent water; cucumbers and watermelons are over 90 percent water. By eating more raw fruits and vegetables, you will be consuming more water.

Action Step:

The 14-Day Vegan Challenge

For the next 2 weeks, consume only plant-based foods such as fruits, vegetables, nuts, and seeds, and eliminate dairy, eggs, meat, and fish. Choose organic fruits and vegetables whenever possible. Record the way you feel each day in your journal by writing down your energy level, motivation, and overall mood. Give yourself this 2-week vegan trial and decide what changes you will make to your diet.

Important tip: Use the app Cronometer to keep a food diary, calculate a nutritional report, and add new recipes.

CREATE A DAILY SPIRITUAL PRACTICE

Self-care is also about spiritual nourishment. Since recovery is an inside job, we benefit immensely from a daily spiritual practice. You've got your exercise plan in place, now it's time for your "innercise" plan. Remember, spirituality is not about religion. Compassion, love, and kindness are universal to all human beings. Spirituality is the absence of dogma. Spiritual practices are simply a way to maintain a connection to a power greater than yourself, whether you call it God, Universe, Higher Power, the Field, the Divine, Nature, or whichever name you choose. Being a highly sensitive person in recovery makes my daily spiritual practice mandatory. When I don't take time for my spiritual practices, I feel disconnected from God, people, and myself. I can be standing among a large group of people and feel completely alone. It's only after I've done my spiritual practices that I begin to feel a deeper connection with others. Your daily spiritual practice might consist of mindfulness and meditation, deep breathing, prayer, a gratitude list, yoga, faith rituals, or any other practices you enjoy.

BEING AN EMPATH IN RECOVERY

Although some components of addiction are genetic and environmental (such as being raised by alcoholic parents), being an Empath can play a significant role.[26]

Judith Orloff, MD

I am a highly sensitive person. Being a highly sensitive person means I can feel the energy around me. When I walk into a meeting or log into a Zoom event, I immediately pick up the energy in the room. According to *The Empath's Survival Guide* by Judith Orloff, here are some characteristics of an empath:

You seem to attract people who want to share their problems with you.

You are easily overstimulated.

You can be extremely vulnerable at times and feel very deeply about an issue or a person.

You need alone time to recharge your inner battery.[27]

Being a highly sensitive person in recovery is a strength. We need more empathy and compassion towards people struggling with addiction and mental health conditions. We truly are the ones we've been waiting for. Growing up, I thought being highly sensitive was a weakness, so I did my best to hide my sensitivities. People told me I was shy and quiet, but I had plenty of thoughts, feelings, and ideas to share. I started to shut off my sensitivities with drugs and alcohol as a teenager and into my early twenties. Today I honor who I am.

After talking to thousands of people in addiction recovery, I find that many of us are highly sensitive people. If you are a highly sensitive person, you need to own this fact about yourself. The way you feel is valid, and you're not crazy. You just need to pay extra special attention to your needs and use self-care tools to survive in this world.

Being in nature is one of my favorite activities as a highly sensitive person. A forest is a place I feel safe and comfortable. I often take off my shoes to ground myself to the earth. Water is also very healing to me. Waterfalls, rivers, oceans, and streams all produce feelings of peace, joy, and excitement. I run a mini waterfall next to my desk every day when I'm working.

Back in June 2020, I was faced with the decision of whether I was going to continue my path as an entrepreneur in recovery. Instead of becoming fearful and anxious, I let my heart and intuition guide me to the next right action. The message I received was to be calm and start practicing twenty-minute rest periods every day. I continued listening to my heart to receive more information about my situation. The solution became clear; what I needed was a deeper dive into my self-care practices and to practice more forgiveness. I needed to forgive the people in the world who are not being forthright with their actions. I needed to forgive my dad for not being there. I needed to forgive myself for holding onto the past. I slowly noticed my reactions to family, friends, and strangers were calmer and more compassionate. I stopped matching the fear-based, negative energy around me and stayed focused on my own energy. Each day became a little easier than the next.

Action Step:

Honor your sensitivities. Schedule alone time and set boundaries in your relationships by limiting the time you spend around people. Write down activities that bring you joy and begin practicing one activity per day.

BREATHING

On average, a person takes around twenty thousand breaths per day.[28] Breathing is life. We must breathe or we will quickly find our end. The people I've encountered in addiction recovery tend to be shallow breathers. I was one of them. Being mindful of your breathing creates a space to pause before responding and helps you remain calm. Practice taking deep heart-centered breaths around difficult people or situations. A technique I use to reduce stress and improve my decision-making abilities is heart-centered breathing. This will help you relax in just a few minutes.

Action Step:

Practice taking deep heart-centered breaths.

Here are the steps:

Begin to focus your attention on your heart. Breath in for 5 seconds, hold for 5 seconds, now breathe out for 7 seconds. You can also check out step one of the Quick Coherence technique to practice breathing with heart focus in the next section.

Suggestion: Place a few fingers or hands on your heart while you practice heart-centered breathing.

MINDFULNESS

We need to slow down to go faster.

Source Unknown

Mindfulness, which is sometimes referred to as silence, stillness, contemplation or meditation, is what brings my daily spiritual practice together. Our mind and bodies in early recovery are often full of stress, anxiety, and fear. Practicing mindfulness helps us quiet the incessant mental chatter and become the observer. It enables us to be in the present moment. Over the last few years, my mindfulness practice has gone through many evolutions. My first introduction to mindfulness through meditation came from my friend Pete. Pete introduced me to a nine-minute guided meditation I listened to every day for a year.

When I took nine minutes in the morning to meditate, I noticed I responded differently to coworkers and customers. For example, my manager would often stress about the demands of her superiors. This stress would transfer to the team, which made me angry and confrontational. When I started meditating daily, I stopped reacting to her. Instead of being triggered, I offered support to her and the team. This eventually led to my promotion to management. Who knew a nine-minute meditation would be this effective?

Coherence techniques and meditation also increase intuition. It's not uncommon to receive an intuitive message during or after a meditation. For example, the name "Entrepreneurs in Recovery" came to me during a meditation. Meditation increases my awareness of subtle messages I might have missed throughout the day, such as a license plate that reads "FORGIVE," or a bald eagle sitting on a branch. Instead of browsing social media or watching television, take ten minutes to practice meditation or a coherence technique.

George Petersen is a close friend I met along my recovery journey. He's a great example of what meditation, yoga, and the 12 Steps can do for your recovery. I met George during his many relapses with IV heroin use. George was given a life-changing opportunity to attend the Chopra Center to become a Vedic educator and meditation instructor in early recovery. George attributes his success in recovery to discovering meditation and teaching it to others. He now runs a company teaching people how to meditate, perform yoga, and eat mindfully. George recently celebrated nine years of long-term recovery.

When I take time for mindfulness, I become calm and centered. I become the observer of my thoughts and not the thoughts themselves. Even when thoughts are racing through my head, I continue to breathe and observe. I'm not perfect at it. On days I don't meditate, normal situations become overwhelming. So, if I miss my mindfulness practices in the morning, I take ten to twenty minutes during the day to practice.

How do I practice mindfulness?

I begin with meditation. My couch is my dedicated meditation spot. I highly recommend you find your own meditation spot. My first action is to sit down on my couch and get comfortable. I place my cell phone on airplane mode and begin taking slow heart-centered breaths. I hit play on a guided meditation of my choice. You can find guided meditations on the app Insight Timer. The goal of meditation is not to stop your thoughts, but simply to observe what's happening. My guided meditation lasts between five and fifteen minutes.

I follow up the guided meditation with the Quick Coherence technique from the HeartMath Institute. The benefits of heart coherence can include faster recovery from physical, mental, and emotional stressors as well as connecting with your intuition.[29] [30] You can use the Quick Coherence technique with your eyes opened or closed. If it feels comfortable, place a few fingers or your hand over your heart while you practice this technique.

The Quick Coherence Technique™

Step 1. Focus your attention in the area of the heart. Imagine your breath is flowing in and out of your heart or chest area, breathing a little slower and deeper than usual.

Suggestion: Inhale 5 seconds, exhale 5 seconds (or whatever rhythm is comfortable).

Step 2. Make a sincere attempt to experience a regener-tive feeling, such as appreciation or care for someone or something in your life.

Suggestion: Try to re-experience the feeling you have for someone you love, a pet, a special place, or an accomplishment, or focus on a feeling of calm or ease.[31]

Action Step:

Practice the Quick Coherence technique or choose a guided meditation to listen to every day for the next 30 days. Aim for a minimum of 5 minutes per day. For those who say, "I don't have time for mindfulness," the Quick Coherence technique can be done in as little as 1 minute.

PRAYER

If the only prayer you ever said in your life
was thank you, that would suffice.

Meister Eckhart

When I was a kid, I used to pray my mom would live until she was 110 years old. I feared losing her, so I would negotiate with God every day. As a teenager, I stopped praying. When my addiction to drugs and alcohol grew worse, my prayers were requests and demands to not be pulled over by a cop, or when I did get pulled over to not to be hauled off to jail. During my court case, I prayed every morning and every night. In the morning I prayed to my Creator (Higher Power, Divine, Source) to keep me away from drugs and alcohol, followed by a request for my freedom. At night, I said a prayer of gratitude for another day of recovery and all the people supporting me.

Today, my prayers start by thanking a Power greater than myself and everyone looking out for me. I give thanks for the opportunity to run my own business and for all the people supporting me, including my family, friends, and recovery team. I pray for the still suffering people that they may find recovery and support.

Each moment is a prayer.

Gregg Braden

Don't let the idea of prayer freak you out. Prayer is a triggering word for some people because it brings up religious ideas, old programming, or bad experiences at 12-Step groups or religious ceremonies. Prayer is a technique for anyone who chooses to use it. Some people use prayer to set intentions or state their gratitude for being alive. If you're not exactly where you want to be at this moment, it's okay to say a prayer for your future and well-being. If prayer does not sit well with you, simply skip it, or just say thank you before bed and thank you when you wake up.

Action Step:

Upon rising, thank your Higher Power, Nature, Source, Spirit, Divine, or whatever name you choose for another day of recovery. Before going to sleep, say thank you again. Use prayer in a way that works best for you.

Important tip: Send appreciation to every person you meet today.

Now it's time to build your daily self-care routine.

BUILD YOUR DAILY SELF-CARE ROUTINE

How do you put all of this together into a daily self-care routine that works for you? Here is my daily routine. Note: I've been practicing my morning routine for many years, so I don't expect you to do everything I do.

The first thing I do when I wake up is make my bed, drink from my water bottle, and do five minutes of stretching. I head to the bathroom sink and splash cold water on my face and brush my teeth. Next, I head to my meditation spot. My meditation spot already has my pen, journal, and books waiting for me. I start by listening to a guided meditation on my phone for about five to fifteen minutes. I follow this with the Quick Coherence Technique for five to ten minutes. When this is complete, I grab my journal and write down my intentions for the day, three to five things I'm grateful for, and what I love and appreciate about myself. I read a few pages from a book then repeat an affirmation. My morning routine is complete. My next action is usually a cold shower.

My evening routine helps me wind down for the day and get ready to sleep. I write my to do list in my planner for the next day and review my goals. After shaving, flossing, brushing, and washing, my next action is to head to my bedroom. I pick up my journal and fill out The FEARS journal. Next, I get on my knees and say my prayers. I occasionally practice a short meditation before I pray. I get into bed and read a few pages from a book before lights out.

Action Step:

Reflect on your takeaways, learnings, and actions from this chapter.

What are 2–3 self-care practices you will start doing immediately to help support your recovery?

1.

2.

3.

What are 2–3 self-care practices you will continue doing immediately to help support your recovery?

1.

2.

3.

What are 2–3 unhealthy habits you will STOP doing immediately to help support your recovery?

(Examples: smoking, procrastination, fast food)

1.

2.

3.

Who will help keep you accountable?

1.

2.

3.

My Morning Routine Self-Care Actions:

1.

2.

3.

4.

5.

My Evening Routine Self-Care Actions:

1.

2.

3.

4.

5.

Bonus: I've included The FEARS Journal in the back of the book. You can use The FEARS Journal to track your progress with the FEARS recovery toolkit. It is designed to capture breakthroughs, adversities, wins, synchronicities, lessons, healing, and gratitude. Go to The FEARS Journal now for the next action step.

Every day, ask yourself: What's one thing I can do, no matter how small, that will improve my self-care?

CHAPTER 10

WHAT I CAN'T DO ALONE, WE CAN DO TOGETHER

*People who say it cannot be done
should not interrupt those who are doing it.*

George Bernard Shaw

Recovery is a lifelong journey of growth, healing, and transformation. Many of us still have old tapes playing in our heads about the past, the stigma we face with mental health conditions and addictions, and the difficulties of the road ahead. I want to remind you that the difficulties you faced, the poor choices you made, and the adversities you've overcome are all part of a greater purpose to serve others. Nothing is wasted. You will free yourself and deeply impact others by sharing your experiences and practicing a program of recovery. The past no longer owns me, and it doesn't have to own you.

If you're reading this book, this might be your second, third or fourth chance. Don't let anyone or anything hold you back. Oftentimes the only thing holding us back is ourselves. We no longer have a need for separation and competitiveness. When we band together to embrace a world of collaborative recovery, the possibilities are endless.

Addiction is the best thing that ever happened to me because I found recovery. Recovery became a lens for me to see the world in new ways. I've been blessed with an opportunity to know myself at a deep, intimate level out of necessity. For the first time in my life, I feel comfortable in my own skin.

For those in active addiction, your life may seem impossible right now. The torture and mental anguish of going even a single day without your solution is unbearable. Reach out for help, and give yourself permission to heal from the grip of your addiction. Recovery is possible. The more you practice the ideas I offer in this book, the more you'll learn about yourself. When old patterns reappear and the pain of the past returns, rely upon your self-care practices, reach out to your recovery team, help someone else, and journal your experiences. Day by day, you'll begin to pursue your recovery as hard as you pursued your addiction.

I'm a recovery warrior. My hardest battles have already been won. Being arrested became my bottom. I was not going to stop using drugs and alcohol, but the threat of losing my freedom and the love of people who supported my recovery made me willing to change. If you've hit bottom, that means you get to start over. The only place to go is up. Does someone need to hit bottom to start changing their life? I don't believe so. Hitting bottom looks different for everyone. You may not have hit bottom, but you might be at a place where enough is enough and feel it's time to make a change in order to reach your true potential.

I don't prefer to label myself as an addict, a felon, or an alcoholic. I'm a person in recovery. Now that you've made it to the end of the book, your journey of discovery and recovery has begun. The world is waiting to hear about your version of recovery. *If not you, then who?* Just don't expect a lifetime of negative thoughts, choices, and habits to go away overnight. To see results from this book, you must do the work and trust the process.

Why do some people get to experience recovery while others do not? Shame, stigma, privilege, pain, corruption, trauma, access to treatment, and lack of treatment options are a few of the reasons. But we have the power as a recovery collective to change this by sharing resources, collaborating, and sharing our recovery stories. The mainstream media doesn't cover this story yet. It's now time to provide accessible, affordable, and holistic treatment options to everyone who asks for help. Our voices will be heard.

The world still doesn't know what to do with all the so-called addicts, alcoholics, and people struggling with addiction and mental health. For those of us who know recovery is possible, let's change the conversation around addiction. My friend Pete and I gave a presentation on the tools we use to help our recovery at a local hospital a few years back. As we walked out of the hospital, Pete received a message about an old friend of ours who had just overdosed and was in the same hospital. We made our way back inside and spent our next hour and a half in conversation. We walked around our friend's hospital unit as he pushed his IV machine around. This man was fortunate to be alive. Many of us know someone whose life has been cut short from addiction. I choose to share recovery out loud for this reason.

A few months after I left my job, I had the opportunity to learn the skill of facilitation from my mentor Jon Berghoff and his company, XCHANGE. In XCHANGE's language, I am helping to unlock collective strengths, resources, and recovery at scale. My recovery facilitation starts with building psychological safety. There are two important factors for psychological safety to happen: all voices must be heard, and the group must be willing to take risks. It becomes a *virtuous* cycle—people will take more risks when they feel safe, feel like they belong, and know their voice is welcome.

My work today is helping to build communities of recovery. I've facilitated thousands of conversations through workshops and events at sober living residences, addiction and mental health treatment centers, recovery/drug courts, recovery community organizations, nonprofits, and professional and peer recovery coach training companies. This didn't happen overnight. It took two years before I landed a significant facilitation opportunity, which came in June 2019, when I connected with Neil Campbell, the CEO of the Georgia Council on Substance Abuse (GCSA). After a series of conversations, Neil hired me to run a six-hour training with a team of leaders from Georgia's recovery community. This training resulted in their decision to hire me to facilitate a large event in Atlanta, Georgia, with thirty different recovery community organizations (RCOs) throughout the state of Georgia. We called this event the RCO Appreciative Recovery Summit. Over one hundred people participated in life-giving conversations as participants connected to their purpose, inner strengths, and top actions for each RCO in 2020.

Afterwards, I received a grant from the GCSA to continue working with Georgia's thirty-four recovery community organizations. I was also hired to facilitate three full-day trainings to over 350 peer recovery coaches called certified addiction recovery empowerment specialists (CARES). Due to COVID-19, I facilitated all of these events online. Neil recently shared with me how these events were the one stable constant the GCSA team and RCO network could all look forward to during the pandemic. The Georgia Council on Substance Abuse is doing groundbreaking work in the field of addiction recovery for the state of Georgia. GCSA has created a platform for the rest of our country to model. You can learn more about GCSA at gasubstanceabuse.org.

My intention today is to continue working with every state in the U.S. so that no person is left behind. I've had the honor to train hundreds of people in recovery facilitation. People in addiction recovery want to do work that ignites their passion. When you facilitate conversations in the addiction recovery world, you realize that people come up with much better answers together than we could ever come up with alone. What's needed is a safe environment where all voices are being heard so that people can be vulnerable and respond to relevant, life-giving questions.

What will be unlocked through your recovery? If you're ready to learn recovery facilitation, there's never been a more important time. Please contact me if you're interested in my next recovery facilitation training.

Today I see a world where every single person is in recovery. Your recovery might be from drugs, alcohol, smoking, gambling, technology, work, sex, trauma, old worn-out beliefs, codependency, food, hate, power, separation, or fear. As a society, we like to point fingers and label people as "addicts." This behavior allows our ego to feel a sense of power and worthiness, but the reality is we are all addicts. We are born into addiction. A study from five years ago found that the average teenager now spends up to nine hours a day on their technology.[32] How much has this increased with social distancing and lockdowns? Addiction has become the norm.

Are you ready?

Now it's your turn to experiment with the FEARS recovery toolkit. Use the FEARS recovery toolkit in combination with your current recovery plan. Start by rereading each of the FEARS chapters and completing the actions. Keep a journal with you and update it every day on what's working. I strongly recommend finding an accountability partner to go through the FEARS recovery toolkit together. Your goal is to go through the process, not to complete it. Your recovery journey is never complete.

Here's a quick overview of the FEARS recovery toolkit:

Focus on Your Recovery

Create a Daily To-Do List
- Action: Use a daily planner and write a daily to-do list for the next 30 days.

Build Your Recovery Team
- Action: Choose 3–5 people to be on your recovery team.
- Action: Reach out to your new recovery team within the next 24 hours.

Keep Yourself Accountable in Recovery
- Action: Ask your recovery team for permission to check in with them daily, as needed.

Finding Purpose in Recovery
- Action: Create your recovery purpose statement.
- Action: Answer clarifying questions about your purpose in recovery.

Elevate Your Recovery

Elevate Your Knowledge
- Action: Read or listen to 5 pages a day.
- Action: Consider a 12-Step program.

Elevate Your Circle
- Action: Choose your 5 mentors.

Elevate Your Vision
- Action: Practice my guided visualizations.

Elevate Your Goals and Intentions
- Action: Create a vision board.

Appreciate Your Recovery

Start Your Day with Gratitude
- Action: Create a daily gratitude journal.

Appreciate Your Self-Talk
- Action: Write down and repeat your affirmations.

Appreciate Your Story
- Action: Write down the people you need to forgive in your journal.

Write Your Story
- Action: Write down your recovery story.

Share Your Story
- Action: Share your story with a support group, recovery friend, sponsor or mentor.

Resilience in Recovery

Leverage Your Inner Power
- Action: Write down your most important goal, opportunity, or challenge in the next 90 days that will require resilience.

Develop a Resilient Heart and Mind
- Action: Create a 10- to 12-word resilience affirmation.

Face Your Fear
- Action: Do one thing out of your comfort zone today

Trust Your Intuition
- Action: Write down times when you trust your heart, intuition, inner knowing, or gut feelings.

Self-Care in Recovery

Get Moving
- Action: Practice 10 minutes of movement every day.

Take Cold Showers
- Action: Turn the last 10–15 seconds of your shower cold.

Get Sufficient Sleep
- Action: Take 10 minutes to rest.

Nourish Yourself
- Action: Make a smoothie. Make a juice.

Stay Hydrated
- Action: Eat plant-based foods for 2 weeks.

Create a Daily Spiritual Practice

Being an Empath in Recovery

- Action: Schedule alone time, set boundaries, and schedule activities that bring your joy.

Breathing

- Action: Practice heart-centered breathing.

Mindfulness

- Action: Practice the Quick Coherence technique or a guided meditation for 30 days.

Prayer

- Action: Say a prayer upon waking and before bed.

Build Your Daily Self-Care Routine

- Action: Reflect on takeaways, learnings, and actions from this chapter.
- Action: Create a morning and evening self-care routine

The FEARS Journal

- Action: Fill out The FEARS Journal at the end of the day for the next 30 days

---

FINAL Action Step:

Complete the 30-Day FEARS challenge. For the next 30 days, make a commitment to complete one action step in the FEARS recovery toolkit each day. Here is a possible example for the first seven days:

Day One: Write down your recovery actions in daily planner

Day Two: Build your recovery team

Day Three: Complete your purpose statement

Day Four: Read or listen to 5 pages of a book

Day Five: Choose your 5 mentors

Day Six: Practice my guided visualization

Day Seven: Create your vision/intention board

Don't overwhelm yourself. If you need to practice each action for a few weeks before moving on, then do it. Be sure to track your progress in your journal.

When you embark on this journey, amazing things start to happen. You will meet the right people at the right time, you'll find a book at the exact moment you need it, or you'll hear a message you need to hear. When things don't go your way, you can take a breath and try again. What's been driving my success? What's made me feel worthy of continuing on my path? It's messages like this one I recently received from a woman who runs a large nonprofit assisting young people with addiction. On our first call together, she opened the conversation by saying, "I have a message to share with you. You are a light in the dark field of addiction. I'm an intuitive person, and that's what came to me." Messages like this keep me focused when I start to doubt myself. We are all the light in the darkness of addiction.

LET'S SHINE OUR LIGHT TOGETHER.

Congratulations on completing this book. If you need help and support, visit www.JesseHarless.com/Coaching.

If this book has impacted you, would you do me a favor and give a copy away to someone else?

Did you work on your FEARS today? I want to hear your FEARS experiences and story. Please send me an email at jesse@jesseharless.com or join the FEARS community on Facebook.

Visit www.myfearscommunity.com to join the Facebook group.

You can sign up for email updates by visiting workonyourfears.com.

THE FEARS JOURNAL

The purpose of The FEARS Journal is to keep track of your recovery progress. The FEARS Journal pulls together my self-care routine and my day. It is designed to capture breakthroughs, adversities, wins, synchronicities, lessons, healing, and gratitude. You can complete The FEARS Journal at the end of the day in as little as 5 minutes.

The FEARS Journal includes the following:

Focus: How did I focus on my recovery today?

1.

2.

Elevate: How did I elevate my recovery today?

1.

2.

Appreciate: How did I appreciate my recovery today?

1.

2.

Resilience: How did I build resilience and/or get out of my comfort zone today?

1.

2.

Self-Care: How did I practice self-care in recovery today?

1.

2.

Here's an example:

Focus:

1. Today I spent an hour talking to Pete.
2. I spoke to Snook about his trip to Montana.

Elevate:

1. Today I listened to *The Untethered Soul* for 10 minutes.
2. I watched *My Octopus Teacher*.
3. I listened to a helpful video on YouTube about earthing.

Appreciate:

1. I appreciate Mom for her support, Nick for our conversation, and George for his passion.
2. I'm grateful for my recovery.

Resilience:

1. Today I stayed focused on writing my book despite feeling tired.
2. I did not let anyone drain my energy today.

Self-Care:

1. I spent 20 minutes walking barefoot outside.
2. I stretched in the morning and worked out in the afternoon.

3. I made a juice with strawberries, watermelon, and lemon.

After I fill out the template above, I capture any additional key lessons, stories, breakthroughs, or learnings throughout the day.

For example:

"What stood out in the book *Heart Intelligence* is that the heart communicates with the brain more than the brain communicates with the heart. What's been helping me through this COVID-19 lockdown is being of service and connecting on Zoom calls. I've never been more excited to connect with new people, even if it's just to answer questions."

Action Step:

Fill out The FEARS Journal at the end of the day for the next 30 days on the template provided. You can also capture any additional inspiration, challenges, and breakthroughs in your journal.

Optional: Share your FEARS journal entries with someone on your recovery team.

Focus: How did I focus on my recovery today?

1.

2.

Elevate: How did I elevate my recovery today?

1.

2.

Appreciate: How did I appreciate my recovery today?

1.

2.

Resilience: How did I build resilience and/or get out of my comfort zone today?

1.

2.

Self-Care: How did I practice self-care in recovery today?

1.

2.

Important tip: Once you've practiced journaling for a year, take a look at your journal entry from a year ago today. This habit will allow you to see your growth in real time. Since we easily forget how far we've come, this is proof we are growing in our recovery. Don't worry if you're just starting out; your goal is to save your journals from now on so you can reference them in the future.

**To download a free copy of The FEARS Journal, go to
www.WorkOnYourFears.com**

NOTES

1   Facing Addiction with NCADD, *Multiple Pathways of Recovery: A Guide for Individuals and Families* 2018, http://www.williamwhitepapers.com/pr/dlm_uploads/Multiple-Pathways-of-Recovery-Guide-2018.pdf.

2   Maia Szalavitz, "How Childhood Trauma May Make the Brain Vulnerable to Addiction, Depression," *Time*, August 1, 2012, https://healthland.time.com/2012/08/01/how-childhood-trauma-may-make-the-brain-vulnerable-to-addiction-depression/.

3   Peter A. Levine, *Healing Trauma: A Pioneering Program for Restoring the Wisdom of Your Body* (Boulder, CO: Sounds True, 2008), 55.

4   Veronique Mead, "Books and Therapies for Healing Nervous System Reponses to Stress, Trauma and Perceptions of Threat," *ACEs Connection*, January 25, 2018, https://www.acesconnection.com/blog/books-and-therapies-for-healing-nervous-system-responses-to-stress-trauma-and-perceptions-of-threat.

5   Gary Wilson, *Your Brain on Porn: Internet Pornography and the Emerging Science of Addiction* (United Kingdom: Commonwealth Publishing, 2014), 64.

6   Matt Morrissey, "How Early Porn Exposure Traumatizes Boys and Fuels Toxic Masculinity," *Fight the New Drug*, April 17, 2019, https://fightthenewdrug.org/matt-morrissey-how-porn-exposure-traumatizes-boys/?utm_source=email&utm_medium=organic&utm_campaign=themovement&utm_term=may.

7   "Porn Releases the Same Chemicals in Your Brain as Cocaine," *A City Free From Porn*, August 27, 2020, https://cityfree.org.au/view/releases-the-same-chemicals-in-the-brain-as-cocaine/.

8   Samantha J. Heintzelman and Laura A. King, "Routines and Meaning in Life," *Personality and Social Psychology Bulletin* 45, no. 5 (September 18, 2018): 688–99, https://journals.sagepub.com/doi/full/10.1177/0146167218795133.

9   Donald L. Hilton, Jr., "Pornography Addiction – A Supranormal Stimulus Considered in the Context of Neuroplasticity," *Socioaffective Neuroscience & Psychology* 3, (July 19, 2013), 207–67, https://www.ncbi.nlm.nih.gov/pmc/articles/PMC3960020/.

10 Gary Wilson, *Your Brain on Porn: Internet Pornography and the Emerging Science of Addiction* (United Kingdom: Commonwealth Publishing, 2014), 63.

11 Bronnie Ware, *The Top Five Regrets of The Dying* (Carlsbad, CA: Hay House, 2011), 47.

12 Bill Wilson and Dr. Bob Smith, *Alcoholics Anonymous: The Story of How Many Thousands of Men and Women Have Recovered from Alcoholism* (New York: Alcoholics Anonymous World Services, 1976), 97.

13 Jack Canfield, *The Success Principles: How to Get from Where You Are to Where You Want to Be* (New York, NY: HarperCollins, 2015), 27.

14 Russell Brand, Recovery: *Freedom from Our Addictions* (London: Bluebird, 2017), 229.

15 James Clear, "How to Build New Habits by Taking Advantage of Old Ones," *James Clear*, November 17, 2020, https://jamesclear.com/habit-stacking.

16 Kamal Ravikant, *Love Yourself Like Your Life Depends On It* (CreateSpace, 2012), 29.

17 Diane Coutu, "How Resilience Works," *Harvard Business Review*, September 15, 2020, https://hbr.org/2002/05/how-resilience-works.

18 Cary Elizabeth Dakin, "The Role of the Intuitive Function in Addiction Recovery" (PhD diss., Pacifica Graduate Institute, 2014), 258, https://pqdtopen.proquest.com/pubnum/3613771.html.

19 Jaime Hope, *Habit That!: How You Can Health Up in Just 5 Minutes a Day* (Austin, Texas: Lioncrest Publishing, 2018), 13.

20 P. C. Dinas et al., "Effects of Exercise and Physical Activity on Depression," *Irish Journal of Medical Science* 180, (2011): 319–25, https://link.springer.com/article/10.1007/s11845-010-0633-9.

21 Nikolai A. Shevchuk, "Adapted Cold Shower as a Potential Treatment for Depression," *Medical Hypotheses* 70, no. 5 (2008): 995–1001, https://doi.org/10.1016/j.mehy.2007.04.052.

22 Geert A. Buijze et al., "The Effect of Cold Showering on Health and Work: A Randomized Controlled Trial," PLoS One 11, no. 9 (2016): 1, https://www.ncbi.nlm.nih.gov/pmc/articles/PMC5025014/.

23 Harvard Health Publishing, "Sleep and Mental Health," *Harvard Mental Health Letter*, October 13, 2020, https://www.health.harvard.edu/newsletter_article/sleep-and-mental-health.

24 X. Wang X. et al., "Fruit and Vegetable Consumption and Mortality from All Causes, Cardiovascular Disease, and Cancer: Systematic Review and Dose-Response Meta-Analysis of Prospective Cohort Studies," *BMJ*, (July 29, 2014): 349, https://www.bmj.com/content/349/bmj.g4490.full.pdf+html.

25 "Intake of Raw Fruits and Vegetables Is Associated With Better Mental Health Than Intake of Processed Fruits and Vegetables," *Front. Psychol.*, (April 10, 2018): 1, https://www.frontiersin.org/articles/10.3389/fpsyg.2018.00487/full.

26 Judith Orloff, *The Empath's Survival Guide: Life Strategies for Sensitive People* (Boulder, CO: Sounds True, 2018), 58.

27 Judith Orloff, *The Empath's Survival Guide: Life Strategies for Sensitive People* (Boulder, CO: Sounds True, 2018), 14-17.

28 Ann Brown, "How Many Breaths Do You Take Each Day?" *The EPA Blog*, April 28, 2014, https://blog.epa.gov/2014/04/28/how-many-breaths-do-you-take-each-day/.

29 HeartMath, *Building Personal Resilience Guide: HeartMath Skills for Personal Effectiveness*, (Boulder Creek, CA: Institute of HeartMath, 2014), 17, https://store.heartmath.com/building-personal-resilience-guide/.

30 Deborah Rozman and Lew Childre, *Transforming Stress: The Heartmath Solution for Relieving Worry, Fatigue, and Tension* (Oakland, CA: New Harbinger, 2005), 20.

31 Doc Childre, Howard Martin, Deborah Rozman, and Rollin McCraty, *Heart Intelligence: Connecting with the Intuitive Guidance of the Heart,* (Cardiff by the Sea, CA: Waterfront Press, 2016), 82.

32 Vicky Rideout, "The Common Sense Census: Media Use by Tweens and Teens," *Common Sense,* 2015, 19, https://www.commonsensemedia.org/sites/default/files/uploads/research/census_researchreport.pdf.

ABOUT THE AUTHOR

Jesse Harless is a leader and facilitator in the addiction recovery and mental health space. As CEO of Entrepreneurs in Recovery®, he facilitates highly experiential online and in-person events that help individuals and organizations harness their strengths and create purposeful visions. Jesse holds a MA in Clinical Mental Health Counseling from Rivier University and is a HeartMath® certified trainer, XCHANGE faculty member, and bestselling author of *Smash Your Comfort Zone with Cold Showers*.

Visit www.JesseHarless.com/contact to order bulk copies or to hire Jesse to speak, train, facilitate, or to hire Jesse as a holistic recovery coach.

Visit www.RecoveryFacilitation.com to learn more about Jesse's recovery facilitation.

Connect with Jesse:

Instagram: @JesseHarless222

Facebook: JesseHarless22

Email: Jesse@JesseHarless.com

Website: JesseHarless.com

INSPIRATION AND IDEAS

INSPIRATION AND IDEAS

Made in the USA
Columbia, SC
12 July 2021

41759722R00085